World War II
The Story Never Told
TOP SECRET

BY

Allen Oxford

First published in The United States in 2024 by
TEP publishing

© The Empire Publishers US, 2024

Text copyright © Allen Oxford, 2024

Cover illustration and design © The Empire Publishers US

The moral rights of the author have been asserted

All rights reserved

No part of this publication maybe reproduced, stored in a retrieval system or transmitted in any form or by any means, without the prior permission in writing of the publisher, nor be otherwise circulated in any form of binding or cover other than that in which it is published and without a similar condition including this condition being imposed on the subsequent purchaser.

THE EMPIRE PUBLISHERS

12808 West Airport Blvd Suite 270M Sugar Land, TX 77478, Unites States

https://www.theempirepublishers.com/

Our books may be purchased in bulk for promotional, educational, or business use.

Please contact The Empire Publishers at +1 844 636-4579, or by email at support@theempirepublishers.com

First Edition December 2024

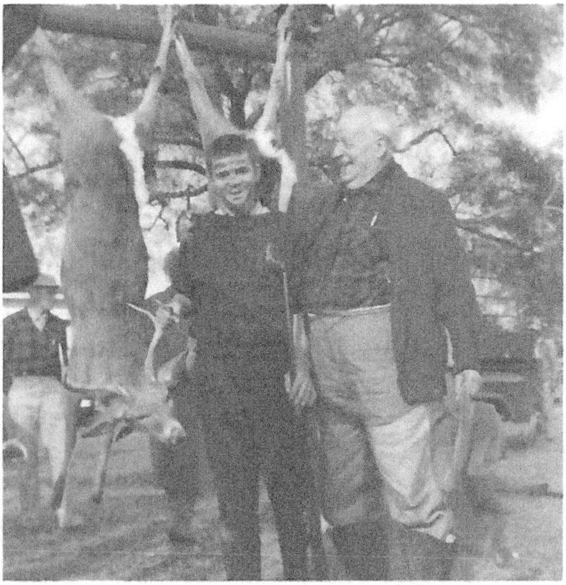

Foreword

I came to be reminded of this story from a short description on a hunt with my Uncle Frank Boykin when I was 16. After reading his memoirs, I decided that the story needed to be told—for if I did not write this book, the story would most likely be lost to history. No leader of any country involved ever admitted that this battle took place. So many other life and death decisions had to be made shortly after this battle, that it got lost in the frantic struggles that followed.

Having no formal writing experience and after a year of research to locate corroborating accounts to reinforce the authenticity of the story, I enlisted several writers to help get the story told in a professional way. My first publication was only about fifty pages, but I felt the story needed more background and depth. It took a village to make that happen.

I hope all who read this book will enjoy learning about a World War II battle that was kept secret for 84 years.

Allen Oxford

Frank William **Boykin** Sr.

(February 21, 1885 – March 12, 1969)

Table of Contents

Prologue 8
Part I The Rise of Frank W. Boykin (1885 - 1916) 15
    The March of Progress 16
    Highs and Lows 25
    Love and War 36
    Up the Ladder 45
    Building an Empire 58
    Taking Chances 71
Part II The Interrim (1906 - 1934) 77
    Winds of Fortune 78
    A Man in Love 89
    Fire, Friends, and Fortune 103
    Prohibition & Opportunity 111
    The Timber Tycoon 123
Part III The Wartime Congressman (1935 - 1943) 130
    Man in Office 131
    Clouds of War 138
    Wisdom in Sorrow 147
    Wolf Across the Channel 158
    The Greek Fire Plan 168
    World on Fire 183
Part IV Epilogue (1944 - 1945) 200

Prologue

It is easy, perhaps, to imagine the scene.

The war had long ended, and the summer clung to Frank William Boykin like a second shirt as he growled out of bed at precisely 5:00 AM. A narrow tweet of birdsong, punctuated by the distant whirr of a motorcar, bounced off the rafters as the Honored Congressman, a man of considerable girth and boundless energy, charged into action like a tank. He wasted no time with pleasantries; the missus, Ocllo Boykin, was already attending to the coffee with a private grumble as her husband reached out to the Dictaphone that was the lifeline of his scattered yet prodigious memory; there was much to be said, and thought and remembered, and the business of the coming hours, days, and weeks could not depend on something as lax as one man's recollection.

No, this was a man who had transformed, at some point, into a whole *system*. As he bellowed into the levered, cold metal of the device, Ocllo would transcribe his coffee-fueled genius would find themselves locked into anything from bureaucratic warfare, to corporate expedition, to the humdrum affairs and issues faced by a singular household that was fortunate enough to have contracted the assistance of the much-beloved Congressman.

As he wolfed down a veritable feast of much-awaited steaming grit, a slice of country ham, eggs, and biscuits begging to be slathered with molasses, Boykin the man was directly in the midst of being Boykin the idea. Here was the patriot's patriot, and between the clatter of silverware and a remarkably elusive recounting of the last session of Congress described for the benefit of an absent party, Boykin embodied his role. Even meals, for him, were social events—even when the only company was the crackling ring from the black rotary phone mounted on the kitchen wall.

With a flourish, one imagines, he must have snatched the receiver off the hook, answering questions about scheduled events and inquiring about sprained ankles with the same cheerful, hectic warmth. He spoke with a thick Alabama drawl, his voice a honeyed blend of molasses and charm as he spoke to his constituents and inquired after the health of grandchildren, the progress of local crops, and the latest gossip with an enthusiasm that could only be described as infectious. There were invitations to be sent, calls from firemen seeking promotions, farmers seeking crop subsidies, and a reminder call from his assistant lining up his tasks for the day. Boykin listened patiently to each call, his booming voice a constant interjection that directed the conversation. By the time the first rays of sunlight slanted through the kitchen window, Boykin had finished his breakfast and his phone calls.

As he dressed and prepared for yet another fully booked day, this first call of the day would, inevitably, just be the first of many—yet luckily, Boykin, the quintessential Southern gentleman, possessed an uncanny ability to remember the names and ailments of seemingly every constituent in Mobile's sprawling first district. Even here in Washington, the heart of the nation's bureaucratic calculus, he had no shortage of friends and colleagues; he was, after all, gregarious by nature and personable by choice.

Now prepared, one can imagine how our extraordinary protagonist looked: a man pushing six feet and with a set of lungs well-suited for lively disagreement, he was a walking, talking explosion of color and texture. Eschewing the typical somber suits that dominated the halls of Congress, Boykin embraced flamboyance—a custom-tailored suit, likely woven from the finest broadcloth, hugged his ample frame. The white vest piping gleamed against the vibrance of his crimson necktie, and a pair of horn-rimmed glasses perched on his wide nose, held in place by a thick black ribbon. Then, adorning his wrists was an impressive array of gold and gem-studded bangles, each one likely a token of lodge membership. Finally, upon his crown was a receding mane of white hair—short, thick, and curiously vibrant in a snowy fashion. With strong, ruddy hands, he slicked it back over a high, tall forehead, before pushing it in place under a brown velour hat.

But beneath the flamboyant exterior, a shrewd mind hummed. Boykin, the self-made millionaire, the timber tycoon, the wartime congressman, was a man of contradictions. He was a champion for his district, a tireless advocate who could navigate the labyrinthine bureaucracy of Washington D.C. with the same ease he navigated the cotton fields of his youth. Federal dollars flowed to Mobile like rain after a drought, funding new schools, hospitals, and vital wartime industries—all thanks to Congressman Boykin's relentless lobbying. Sure, there were rumors about him as well—there was controversy, and there were critics, but they rarely worried about the wide smile of the erstwhile Congressman. He had grown up in the south; mosquitoes rarely worried him.

He was a man of talents, yes; a master of the glad-hand and backroom deal, a man who could navigate the halls of Congress with the same ease he steered his timber empire. One moment, he'd be regaling a room full of socialites with tales of his rise from humble beginnings; the next, he'd be locked in a tense negotiation with a powerful industrialist, his voice dropping to a low growl as he hammered out a mutually beneficial agreement. For the people of his constituency, Boykin was a hero—he was their Frank, their champion, one o' their boys. Whether it was securing vital war supplies for the boys overseas or improving the lot of his folk, Boykin always played the game to win.

Now, with a distracted call out to Mrs. Boykin, he was off, pushing apart the grand doors of the hotel he was staying at with a flourish. Unleased like a human hurricane upon the staid streets of Washington D.C, Boykin wasn't one for a subtle entrance. No sir; Congressman Boykin announced his arrival with the gusto of a brass band. Outside, summer had taken a firm grip; women in starched dresses fanned themselves with folded newspapers, sweat clinging to rouged cheeks as their husbands dressed for the summer in light suits, mopped their brows.

He would always spend a moment with a stray dog if he found one waiting; he was fond of dogs and downright devoted. Newspapers referred to him as the dog lover, and for good reason; back in Alabama, his sprawling game preserves housed a pack of many hounds. He was a regular visitor to the district dog pound, and his booming voice was a welcome disruption to the usual clamor. There, he wasn't a Congressman, but a savior; dozens of strays found a new lease on life thanks to Frank's interventions. He had a keen eye for a deserving companion, and would find the perfect match for himself, adding another friend to his pack. But he was also generous, and friends and associates would be unsurprised to find a playful pup on their doorstep, courtesy of the lively congressman. Frank Boykin ensured that love was always shown to his own, and often, it came with a wagging tail or a wet nose.

As he went about his day, more than once, he would take off his hat and point to the phrase embroidered there in gold. One can see it clearly—Boykin pointing to his hat, chuckling as he read the text in his lively accent:

"*Everythin's Made For Love,* see!" he'd say, perhaps, grinning.

And that's who Frank W. Boykin was: a man of idealistic honesty, and yet a man of apparent contradictions. Here was a man from humble beginnings now enrobed in flamboyant clothes and an even more colorful personality. And yet he was more than just a character; he had known the wartime congress, touched every cornerstone of the American zeitgeist as a politician, practiced investment consummately, and created a small industrial empire all of his own.

Ask one of his constituents, and you would have heard this: Frank was a man who embodied the American ideal of the guy pulling himself up by the bootstraps. Ask one of his colleagues, and you would have been told that he was a man who knew what he was about. And if you were to ask a certain oil man named Joe Danziger, he might chuckle and say that Frank W. Boykin was the man who burned Hitler...

Part I

The Rise of Frank W. Boykin

(1885 - 1916)

The March of Progress

The flames of the Civil War still lingered when Frank W. Boykin drew his first breath. Twenty years had passed since Appomattox, yet scars ran deep in Alabama; conflict had ravaged the land.

The war, as wars tend to do, had ended—but the aftermath brought a new paradigm, one of instability. There was scarcely a family untouched by war—a fallen son, a lost limb, a father never to return. Planters, once accustomed to a seemingly endless supply of cheap labor, were left scrambling after the emancipation of the slaves. The price of cotton had plummeted to six cents a pound, and the war had seen the destruction of countless cotton gins, leaving farmers with miles to travel for processing, a harsh obstacle considering the dilapidated state of the roads. With years—long, tired years—improvement would come, of course;

but the interests of the South would remain on the nation's backburner.

The Boykins, to whom Frank was born, represented the breed of men that had, for long years, flourished in the South. Having reached Alabama early in the eighteenth century, their lot had steadily improved; land had multiplied, and fortunes had multiplied likewise. Theirs was a slow growth, but a growth; and even in previous times of strife, growth had continued with a kind of dogged perseverance, one that enmeshed perfectly with the South overall. In the wake of a devastated economy, the Boykins, like many others, had suffered—but a worse time was to come for them, not too far into the future.

Frank was born in 1885 to James Boykin and Glo Ainsworth in Choctaw County, as the fourth of an eventual brood of ten children. Large families were the rule in those days, after all, especially for a sharecropping way of life. Since the collapse of the plantation system after the Civil War left many landowners with vast tracts of land but a severe labor shortage, sharecropping had emerged as a solution. Landowners could divide their land into smaller parcels and offer them to sharecroppers, who would farm the land in exchange for a share of the crops.

Agreements varied, but they generally followed a similar structure. Landowners provided the land, housing (often shacks in poor condition), and sometimes tools and seeds. Sharecroppers, in turn, provided their labor and that of their families, making large families like the Boykins more efficient since they could provide a greater amount of labor. Life on a sharecropping farm was thus one of hard labor and toil; from sunup to sundown, James and his children labored in the fields. The work was tough, with few technological advancements to ease the burden; nonetheless, this hard upbringing acquainted the young Frank from the get-go with a tough, earned work ethic.

His early years passed without great incident; not here yet were marching and trappings of progress; not here yet was the boom; the economy was still at a standstill, and the land was bought and sold at a rate of continuous, disheartening loss per acre. Yet other tracts of land lay heavily, useless under the hot sun and the dry Alabama summer. Though progress continued elsewhere, it trickled slowly into the lives of the Boykins; intangible revolutions in the South were slow revolutions, and the growth of the industry was a steady shuffle instead of a march. The economy stumbled and crawled, and as the American public elsewhere grew bloated with promise and luxury elsewhere, thirty more years would pass before even the telephone reached Choctaw County, Alabama.

Barefoot, thick-haired, and inquisitive, a young Frank entered the Boykin household one day with an air of perplexed curiosity. His father looked at the seven-years-old with mild amusement, before looking away. The young Frank cleared his throat; the neighbor, a nice man all around, had sparked the boy's imagination by telling him there was a new-fangled way to light houses.

"Dad, can y'really light a house without coal-oil or kerosene?"

"Yes, son, y'can. With *electricity*."

The young Frank looked at his father with wonder. "What's *elec-tricity*, Dad?"

"Son," James Boykin shook his head, "I don't figure anybody in the world knows *exactly* what it is. But there's a man named Edison, and see, he invented a lamp, one that burns *electricity* and goes and gives enough light for a house!"

The wonder on young Frank's face slowly morphed into a frown. *Electricity*. It sounded like magic, replacing the familiar, sooty kerosene lamps their small shanty relied on. He pictured an end to the flickering flames, the pungent smell, and the constant worry of fire. This new "electricity" promised something cleaner, brighter. A part of him yearned to see it in action, and a restless energy thrummed beneath his skin—even in so tender an age, Frank Boykin held fire in his palm.

***

But change was finally marching into the Boykin world, though it was not the change that anyone had hoped for or expected. The year was 1893, and the Panic had descended, plunging America into a depression unlike any before. Breadlines snaked for miles in bustling cities, factories stood idle, and the once-optimistic clang of railroad tracks fell silent. Farmers, already burdened by years of hardship, saw their crops plummet in value, pushing many to the very brink of starvation. The South, already cripplingly dependent on cotton, felt the harshest blow as the price of the white gold sunk to a record low of three cents a pound, leaving the cotton belt in a state of utter despair.

The senior Boykin, a farmer with a growing family, found his fortune dwindling with each passing day. With a heavy heart, James Boykin made a decision—to abandon the failing plantation and seek a new beginning in the village of Fairford, forty miles away. The sadness of their unwilling exodus was, however, offset by the optimism of the children. As far as they were concerned, they were on their way to a new world—a better one, surely. Alongside the caravan trotted Jim, Frank's bluetick hound; a love for dogs would follow him for much of his life.

Before and after the family's move to Fairford, Frank's education continued at a rocky pace. His learning was presided over by Miss Ruth, a woman he would later hold in great esteem. Despite this reverence, however, Frank was a challenge to confine; his boundless energy and his inherent wildness clashed with the structured routine of education in the day, and cramming the rebellious child into a schoolroom for eight hours a day was nigh impossible. Frank chafed under the restrictions, a wild energy threatening to burst out at any moment.

Even when the Boykins uprooted themselves and moved to Fairford, Miss Ruth's pursuit to educate Frank continued. Despite the challenges posed by his exuberant nature, under

Miss Ruth's influence, Frank learned the fundamentals—reading, writing, and basic arithmetic. Importantly, she helped him develop his signature: a distinct and flamboyant autograph as unique as the man himself. And while Frank's formal education may have been brief, it laid the groundwork for his future achievements.

But life in Fairford was not easy, and the Boykin fortunes seemed at risk as James Boykin's health began to fail. Prepared to carry his own weight by now, a still-young Frank found employment in a sawmill, and like the rest of his family, Frank redoubled his efforts, doing odd jobs and running to add his own few pennies. One sweltering morning, Frank walked down to the construction site of a new trestle at the Paul Bayou Creek. He went up to the foreman.

"I'm Frank Boykin, lookin' for work. Could y'use a waterboy? It's gettin' mighty hot."

The foreman looked at the small boy, raising an eyebrow. "*Hm.* Well, I reckon I could be usin' one," he drawled. "Sure, y'got somethin' there, young man. But ain't you mighty young? How old are ya?"

"Eight—but I'm strong, an' I don't mind working," asserted young Frank.

"All right," the foreman said, stroking his chin "Right, I'll be takin' you on as waterboy at a whole thirty-five cents a day, whatcha say?"

"I'll take it," Frank beamed.

When Frank made his way home from his first real job, he felt an immense satisfaction. For a while, things proceeded as expected: each trip, he carried a heavy bucket for seven trips back and forth, his arms aching but his will strong. After a few weeks, the foreman contemplated hiring another water boy; Frank, however, had other ideas. The tree gang, he pointed out, consumed twice the water he could carry alone. But Frank wasn't one to back down from a challenge.

"If I can find a way t'double my load," he proposed, "can I keep the extra thirty-five cents?"

The foreman, with a grin, agreed to a trial.

That evening, a determined Frank set to work with his father's tools—a drawknife, a saw, and a seasoned oak board. Two hours later, he was done—he had made a shoulder yoke carved from wood. To this, he attached two short chains, each with a hook on the end, allowing him to simultaneously carry two buckets. This contraption not only doubled his capacity but offered much-needed relief for his weary arms, and as harsh as the days were, they passed under the vigilance of a will that was tested day after day.

And so, as the times marched ahead, young Frank marched ahead along them. His upbringing had given him boundless energy and relentless will and drive, and all three of these aspects were sharpened by the strong, unquestioned faith that kept him and his family going. Many years later, when Frank would sit at the head of a great empire with success after success behind him, he would look back and remember where he had come from, and who he had been—a boy who had something to struggle for, and had the strength of mind to pull it off.

Highs and Lows

The whistle of the train echoed through Fairford, a sound that had excited the young Frank. Now, at fifteen, the train was his livelihood.

Gone were the days of stumbling under buckets; his days were now filled with long hours of hauling supplies, stacking provisions, and cleaning kerosene lamps. The work wasn't glamorous, but the knowledge he gleaned from it was invaluable. Frank soaked up the workings of the steam-powered lure of modernity and the web of trade that the railroad facilitated. He breathed in the logistics of running a commissary and the push-and-pull of supply and demand, and his newfound knowledge ignited yet another spark in Frank; he displayed an uncanny knack for leadership, and by fifteen, he found himself managing a railroad commissary for the Seaboard Manufacturing Company of Kansas City.

It was a baptism by fire—a crew of workers twice his age looked to him for direction. His days started before dawn. He learned to anticipate needs, to balance inventory efficiently, and to negotiate the best prices with suppliers. Every penny counted, and Frank developed a hawk-eyed vigilance and a creativity that would serve him well. At the same time, he took on an extra job as a salesman in the commissary store. Sleep was a luxury he rarely afforded, often doubling as a salesman in the commissary store, ready to close a deal at any hour. Combining his railroad duties with sales, Frank deftly transformed a train car into the largest, cheapest, and singly best-stocked mobile commissary north of Mobile.

Frank would smile as orders poured in; the customers flocked to him, and he was especially pleased with the ladies coming by, ruddy-cheeked with rouge and always staying a little longer than needed. They were enamored with him, and his magnetism did little to dissuade their attentions.

But fortune rises in uneven tides, as Frank would soon discover.

***

One day, Frank as hurried down the dusty road towards the Seaboard commissary store, he found himself arriving around five minutes late. As he entered the rustic store, the manager, a stern man with a sharp tongue, was already waiting, his arms crossed and his expression thunderous.

"What d'ye mean comin' down 'ere t'work at this time in the mornin'?" he bellowed as soon as Frank came into view. "I'm talkin' to you, y'sonuvabitch!"

Frank had never liked a bully—it didn't matter if he was older, bigger, stronger, or richer than him; the very idea of someone trying to break him down sat ill at ease with the fiery young man. And what's more, he had never tolerated insults on his family, and this was about all he could take. Without a second thought, the furious youth swung his fist, and a blow landed square on the manager's chin, sending him staggering backward. The silence that followed was deafening. Frank's heart pounded in his chest as he watched the manager teeter on the edge of consciousness. Then, with a sickening thud, the man's head struck a nearby iron plow.

Frank stared, numb, at the crumpled form splayed unconsciously on the rough wooden floor. Though the man would live, in those days, such a thing was hardly certain; as a flustered Frank left the scene, he worried over what might happen. By nightfall, the woods surrounding Fairford offered the only solace. His father, concerned and worried, found him there, along with a few trusted friends. Already, though the man was alive, rumors were painting Frank as a killer. It was clear that he couldn't stay.

A plan was hastily hatched. Tom Armistead, a black freedman, was hired for the task. In Tom's rickety one-mule wagon, Frank jolted through the moonlit backroads. The rhythmic clopping of the mule's hooves was a stark counterpoint to the frantic drumbeat of his heart. They spoke little, the weight of the situation hanging heavy between them. The fifteen-mile journey to McIntosh, his mother's cousin Oscar Rush's town, seemed to stretch into eternity. Finally, the weary sun peeked over the horizon, casting long shadows across the dusty road. Relief washed over him as Tom pulled the wagon into the heart of McIntosh. Oscar, a burly man with a gruff exterior and a surprisingly kind heart, readily agreed to offer him refuge, and his house became Frank's sanctuary. Yet, the weight of his forced exile gnawed at him; he already craved the familiar routine of work, the camaraderie with his fellow workers. The quiet life, Frank realized, did not suit him.

Idleness, however, was not in his nature. Soon, restlessness gnawed at him. It was then he stumbled upon Cap'n Fletcher Hooks' general store, a ramshackle building crammed with everything from bolts of fabric to pickled pigs' feet. The Cap'n, a wiry old man with a fiery glint in his eyes, was an ardent Confederate. Every evening, after the store doors were firmly shut, he'd regale Frank with tales of past battles, each word dripping with pride and a touch of bitterness.

"We whooped those damn Yankees good," the Cap'n would roar, brandishing a pipe that emitted a plume of pungent smoke. "Sent them running back north with their tails between their legs!"

Frank would listen patiently, a small smile on his lips. But the Cap'n, bless his ramblings, offered more than just war stories. He needed help running the store. Frank, ever resourceful, quickly donned the hat of a triple threat—postmaster, salesman, and general all-around handyman. Though technically, the Cap'n held the official postmaster title; he spent most of his time reminiscing over past glories, leaving Frank to handle the day-to-day operations.

"Wasn't never officially appointed," Frank would say later, a hint of amusement in his voice. "But the mail had to get delivered, didn't it?"

Life in McIntosh settled into a rhythm. Then, one day, as the Alabama sun beat down mercilessly on the small town of Fairford, an old black man shuffled into the Seaboard commissary store. This was "Uncle" Ned Coleman, a fixture in the small town of Pinewood. He earned $2.50 a month delivering mail from the ramshackle post office to the nearby train depot, his weathered face etched with the lines of a life spent under relentless sun.

As Uncle approached, Frank greeted him with a customary nod, but he didn't return it. Instead, the old man shuffled directly to the counter, his gaze fixed on the row of shotguns displayed on the rack behind it. "I want to buy me a shotgun," he grunted without preamble, his voice rough with age and a hint of desperation. "Uhm, maybe that 'un," he pointed to the gleaming firearm hanging on the wall, "I gotta kill me a man. He ran off with my woman, that Jezebel, and what I'm gunna do is that I'm gunna kill 'im. How much is it?"

Frank understood; at this time in the South, taking a man's lady was the worst kind of insult, one that demanded retribution. Selling a gun for such a purpose wouldn't even raise an eyebrow, and Frank had himself a job to do. "Forty dollars," he stated matter-of-factly. "It's one of 'em new ones, see?"

Uncle's shoulders slumped in defeat. "Now see, Mr. Frank, I ain't got no forty dollars. I jest ain't got no fifty cents neither," he admitted, desperation creeping into his voice. "But I sho' do want that gun."

Frank's mind raced as he considered the old man's predicament. Bartering was against Cap'n Hooks' rules, but Frank had a stash of cash hidden away, known only to himself. With a flicker of determination, he made up his mind.

"Now then, what else you got that's worth money?" Frank inquired. "I ain't promisin' nothin', but maybe we could work up a trade."

The old man's eyes lit up with hope. "I got eighty acres o' land near the rail tracks," he confessed. "Been tryna sell it fer years, but ain't nobody wants that no-good patch of dirt."

Eighty acres along the railroad near McIntosh; Frank's mind whirled with possibilities. Despite the land's current lack of value, he saw its potential. With a decisive nod, he agreed to the trade.

"Let's be goin' and takin' a look at it," Frank suggested. Together, they inspected the land, and by the time the sun dipped below the horizon, the deal was sealed. Uncle Ned had his shotgun, and Frank held the deed to eighty acres of land. The old man, clutching the shotgun tightly, hurried off, vengeance etched on his face. In his hand, Frank held the deed to eighty acres of seemingly worthless land—a deed that held the promise of future riches, if his gamble paid off.

True to form, Frank wasted no time in maximizing the value of his new acquisition. He swiftly harvested the land's timber and floated it down to Mobile, where it fetched a handsome price. And even better, in the years to come, this land piece of 'no-good land' would pay for itself many times over.

***

By the age of sixteen, Frank Boykin was eager to return to his upward trajectory. With his name cleared back in Fairford, Frank returned to work. As the calendar pages flipped with agonizing slowness, Frank toiled relentlessly, making it seem easy on the surface. By year's end, when the Seaboard suits finally descended for their sales reckoning, their jaws hit the floor; Frank, a greenhorn with ink barely dry behind his ears, had utterly eclipsed the entire veteran sales force—all fourteen of them. Promotion, now, was inevitable after his audacious success, yet there was a hitch. The older clerks, clutching years of service like war medals, choked on envy; they resented the very thought of being managed by a stripling, a youth still sporting short pants like a child.

But the Seaboard brass, shrewd men who recognized a diamond in the rough, proceeded with the promotion nonetheless, making him a store manager and raising his salary to $30 a month.

"Son," one of them advised before leaving, "You might be better off investing in a pair o' long trousers." Frank, understanding, nodded eagerly, ready to conquer the next frontier. Little did he know, the war had just begun: as he would soon learn, accounting wasn't his strong suit. Frank knew just about as much about bookkeeping as his rabbit hound, and he struggled with invoices, cash balances, and inventory well past midnight, on top of his early morning railroad shift.

One day, a family friend named Dr. Granade offered him some financial advice with remarkable foresight. "Frank," he said, "Yer a wonderful boy, but y'should start a bank account! Why don't y'go to Mobile and deposit a little money every payday, hm? Listen, one o' these days this store is goin' out of business. When this happens, you'll be needing a little something in the bank; with that, you'll be able to go into some business for yourself. Good God be willin', you may even be a wealthy man some day!"

Frank took the advice. On his next payday, he and Dr. Granade traveled to Mobile. As the train rumbled to a stop, he followed Dr. Granade into the imposing building of the People's Bank. Inside, the air hung heavy with the scent of ink and money, and the teller loomed behind a brass grate. Frank deposited his fifteen dollars, and with a clipped voice, the teller gave Frank his first leather bankbook. It wasn't much, just a leatherbound thin sheaf of paper, but it held the weight of his dreams, a seed finally sown in fertile ground.

As Dr. Granade had predicted, time had kept going on, and the march of progress had another victim: the commissary at Fairford, his first taste of independence, was shut down and boarded up. The restless young Frank wasn't one to waste time; he realized that he knew the gist of the business like the back of his hand, and this knowledge would serve him well. Armed thus, Frank Boykin marched straight into the AT&N he'd once left behind. The president, a stern man used to dealing with hardened businessmen, looked down at a fresh-faced youth in ill-fitting clothes—yet, something in Frank's eyes snagged the president's attention. Frank laid out his proposition: he could supply the crossties, the bridge timbers, everything the railroad needed to expand its tracks.

The president saw an opportunity to capture lightning, and Frank saw a chance to sink or swim. And just like that, with a single nod, young Mr. Boykin found himself staring down a mountain of timber. But there was no fear in the fledgling businessman's eyes, because he knew there was no room for fear in the big leagues. This was Frank Boykin's chance, and the stakes had never been higher.

Love and War

The fruits of Frank's ambition coalesced in Calvert. It was here that, with the money earned from the lumber business, Mr. Boykin built the largest and first brick general store in Washington County. As the sun filtered through its new glass windows with a lilting gleam, the store stood solid and proud as a witness to Frank's rising fortunes.

But this was not enough. Ever the savvy businessman, Frank believed in diversification; instead of just stocking shelves, Frank's store curated experiences. From trinkets for wide-eyed children to exotic goods, his emporium became a magnet for curious customers. A booming "Welcome!" would echo from Frank himself as he played the showman, his smile warm as he promised the possibility of finding something *just right* on his shelves. Young, strong, and capable, he knew how to play to an audience; towering above many visitors, he seemed even taller due to his larger-than-life personality. His eyes sparkled with mischief, sometimes from behind round wire-framed glasses. Already, his style was unconventional yet put together; think suspenders, bold patterns, and pocket squares. A master at reading people, Frank had mastered the ability to sell.

But his true genius lay in his ability to tap into the undercurrents of local desire. He took on various side investments, particularly hogs and gamecocks. Hogs, though a common source of profit, paled in comparison to the thriving sport of cockfighting. Market days were often a covert celebration of these avian gladiators, bred for generations like feathered athletes. In makeshift arenas all over the South, weathered and calloused men would gather in a smoky haze of pipe tobacco as wagers were exchanged. After inspection, the birds would be released into the center of the dirt pit until, after a flurry of feathers, a victor would stand over his fallen opponent. Though no lover of the sport itself, Frank noticed how folk came all the way from Mobile to buy his scrappers, and saw a chance to capitalize on the craze himself.

But cockfighting was by far the only side hustle Frank cultivated. His keen eye for opportunity led him to the booming market for Texas Mustangs. He bought them in droves, a hundred at a time, for only $15 a head. Cowboys delivered the wild beasts to a makeshift corral behind his store, where Frank, a master tamer, could break three mustangs a day. Once secured, horses would be quickly gentled, as Frank easily habituated the horse to touch and presence, using his lively and confident nature to desensitize the creatures and ease their skittishness. These tamed beasts would then be sold off for $100 or more, often on a convenient two-year payment plan. This Mustang trade, in turn, led Frank into a lucrative livery service. Double-buggies waited at the Calvert train station, day and night, ready to whisk traveling salesmen, laden with sample trunks, on their county-wide canvassing sprees.

And if there was something Frank Boykin remembered, it was his friends, and those who had done him a good turn. Among these was Tom Armistead, the man who had once helped him escape Fairford, drawing him on a one-mule wagon for 15 miles in the dark. This, Frank knew, was a man who had earned his trust; thus, sending for Tom and his wife, Frank employed him as his porter in Calvert. Appreciative, Tom took quickly to his duties, and Frank would continue to do right by the Armisteads for the rest of his life.

And so, for now, things seemed to be looking up—but things are also never that quite that simple.

***

Among the close friends of the Boykins was Judge Berry Cannon. The good Judge practiced in Mobile County and had a reputation for being strict but fair. He enforced the law and expected respect for it, and as befit the ruggedness of his times, he happened to be the fastest draw in Mobile County. Though the exact number of the duels he fought remained a mystery, one thing was for sure: his word was law, and few dared to challenge him.

Frank's primary interest with the Judge had less to do with the man himself, and everything to do with his daughters, Addie and 'Mike' Cannon. Of course, the Judge had strict rules about courting his daughters. On evenings when Frank came calling with a smile, the Judge, who loved to play the violin (though it hardly the most pleasant music), would play loudly in the next room. One can easily imagine Frank's charismatic gaze lingering on the Cannon sisters as they giggled back, blushing. Addie and Mike were both beautiful, and Frank was sweet on Mike in particular. Spending time with her, Frank hardly minded the Judge's musical interference; however, when the Judge stopped playing his fiddle at exactly nine o'clock, it would be time for Frank to bid farewell once again. And so things continued for a while without much incident.

One warm Saturday night, Frank rode swiftly back from the store, the day's earnings tucked away securely in his saddle bag. Above, the moon hung low in the sky, casting long shadows across the boardwalk with a silver stroke. Just then, three menacing silhouettes emerged from the shadows and opened fire on him. Bullets whizzed past his ears as he frantically tried to protect himself and his money. His horse reared up in fear, almost throwing Frank off its back. In desperation, Frank drew one of the two guns he carried on him at all times, and fired blindly into the darkness, digging his spurs into his steed's flanks as he raced away from certain death. Adrenaline coursed through his veins as he shook his head; stick-ups and muggings had been growing in the area, and though he'd been prepared to be on the receiving end, he still hadn't expected it.

The next morning before daybreak, he boarded a train for his logging business, and two weeks would pass before he returned. The night he returned, he hurried to see "Mike"—but it was the Judge who met him on the porch. With a stern look on his weathered features, the Judge spoke up.

"Be in court at seven the next morning," he said gruffly, without preamble.

"What for?" asked Frank, asked from, disconcerted.

"Well," said the Judge, "One o' the fellas you shot the other night's dead an' buried. I've got you charged with murder."

"But I..."

"You can tell it in court tomorrow," the Judge cut in.

And that was that; Frank knew there was no possibility of arguing with the man. Riding home, Frank resolved not to go to prison. He had built up something for himself, and he'd rather take off for Texas than be imprisoned. To live in a metal box! Such a fate revolted Frank Boykin, and he knew it would ruin his growing business and family. Thinking to himself, he decided that tracking him down in Texas would hardly be easy; he could just stay there for a while, and hopefully, the whole thing might blow over soon.

On his way to court in the morning, he found Mike Cannon waiting for him.

"Frank," she said, seeming worried. "You be very careful with Papa; he's in a right temper today."

"Hol' on, Mike. Listen, what I've decided to go do, is that I'd rather be off down Texas than let 'em put me behind bars for defendin' my life and property," Frank said hotly, before looking at her intently. "But I'd like to take you with me. Got another horse waitin', too. Will you go?"

To his astonishment, the girl replied, "Frank, I'd go anywhere in the world with you."

"Well, best get yourself ready," Frank said. "We may be needin' to leave in a hurry."

Slipping past her, Frank made his way into the courtroom, which hummed in the oppressive heat. Sunlight speared through high, dusty windows, and gleaming mahogany furniture, worn smooth by countless trials, filled the space. The jury, meanwhile, sat in uncomfortable wooden chairs, fans clutched to their brows. The Judge, a man whose gaze could pierce steel while on the job, eyed him down from his throne. Amidst the scent of wood polish and sweat, Frank took the stand, noting the hefty Bible that sat before him.

"Now, what have you got to say for yourself?" the Judge demanded once Frank had taken the oath.

Frank thus laid out his story, the bare-bones account of his survival. He'd shot a man, yes, but only to protect himself and his hard-earned wages. Three figures in the dark, gunfire erupting—what other choice did he have? As he recounted the events, he seemed cool as could be, though a part of him was idly wondering what it'd take to bust his way out, grab Mike, and be on the road to Texas.

He finished, and silence descended. The judge regarded him with a cool intensity; then, the verdict.

"Frank Boykin! *Git!*" The judge roared. " Get out of here, and don't you let this happen again! If you come back into this here court again inside of twelve months, I'll clap you right in jail. Y'understand?"

Relief washed over Frank. "Yes sir! Yes sir!" he nearly shouted.

"Good," the Judge sat back, satisfied. "Now, you get lost and stay lost. Court adjourned!"

Sighing in relief, Frank dashed out; no jail time for him! And best of all, the coming Saturday saw him yet again in the Judge's living room, hair combed back and a smile on his face as he waited for Mike, listening to the violin in the other room!

Up the Ladder

Frank wasn't a man for half-measures. Having secured Calvert as his domain, his general store humming with activity, he craved more.

He craved *expansion*.

Frank's boots thudded a steady rhythm on the wooden planks of the Calvert depot platform. President Cochrane, a portly and sensible man, listened intently as Frank finished his pitch. The air hung heavy with the metallic tang of coal smoke and the rhythmic groan of a distant locomotive.

"So, Mr. Cochrane," Frank concluded, his voice a warm Southern drawl, "Y'see that switchin' your road shops to Calvert would *not only* streamline your operations but also cut costs *sig-nifi-cantly*."

Cochrane steepled his fingers, his gaze flickering over Frank's somewhat eccentric dressing sense. "Intriguing proposition, Mr. Boykin. But a move of that scale requires substantial deliberation."

Frank pressed on, his smile unwilling to show even a crack. "Of course, sir. I wouldn't be expectin' anything less. But consider this—my general store caters *directly* to your workforce. Now, think of what my offer means. No more wastin' time traveling for supplies. And! The quality-of-goods and the credit system I'm offerin' are top of the line. An' that's without me mentioning that I know your folk, and they know Frank. We get along, and there's somethin' to be said about keepin' morale up and running."

Cochrane grunted, a hint of a concession flickering in his eyes. Frank knew he had planted a seed. He'd dealt with men like Cochrane before, and if there was one thing Frank Boykin knew, it was how to plant a seed into a stubborn mind deep enough that it was bound to sprout something up.

Within a year, Frank's gamble had paid off. The Calvert store bustled with activity. The clatter of cash registers and the murmur of conversation filled the air. He knew his customers by name, their families, their needs. He wasn't just a shop owner; he was Frank, a friend, a reliable anchor in their often-uncertain lives.

He wasn't going to rest on his laurels, he decided. Sure, his crosstie operation, currently a steady earner, held the most promise. But how to propel it to new heights? The answer, clear as a mountain outcrop, was the Southern Railroad—the biggest crosstie buyer on the Eastern seaboard. Why chase minnows, he thought, when you could land a whale? But the plan demanded effort, and he spent days practicing his sales pitch, playing to a game of inventor's bingo to list down numbers and promises of quality that would leave him in the railroad barons' good graces.

There was just one hurdle—securing a meeting.

To Washington D.C., Frank decided. The big city in the American heart greeted him with a cacophony of unfamiliar sounds—the blare of car horns, the nasal voices of vendors, and the incessant chatter that was as inane as it was lively. Standing amidst the throng at the old Sixth Street depot, a far cry from the familiar comfort of Calvert, Frank felt a slight pang of doubt. He had a plan—but navigating the labyrinthine world of Washington bureaucracy was a different beast altogether. An idea sparked in his mind. Weren't there Alabama senators in the Capitol? The name of Senator Bankhead came to mind

Hailing a cab, Frank climbed in, his boots leaving a dusty imprint on the worn leather seat. "Take me to Capitol Hill," he instructed the driver, a wiry man with a glint in his eye. The cab rattled and swayed through the uneven streets. Frank soon realized he was being taken for a ride—quite literally. The driver, sensing his naivety, was milking the fare.

"Hey! Ol' boy!" Frank protested, his voice rising above the traffic. "Now, isn't this a bit out the way?"

The driver, feigning innocence, shrugged. "Just showin' you the sights, sir. It's a beautiful city, ain't it?"

By the time they finally reached Capitol Hill, Frank was fuming. The fare, a hefty dollar, felt like a slap in the face. Ten cents was the usual rate, a fact he was now painfully aware of.

But anger was a luxury he couldn't afford; he had a bigger fish to fry. Managing to get an audience with the Senator, Frank met him and shook his hand. "Son," The Senator exclaimed. "why didn't you bring your father with you?"

Frank smiled, unfazed. "Figured I could handle myself jus' fine, sir. I'm Frank Boykin."

A flicker of recognition crossed Fink's face. "The Frank Boykin who been selling all them railroad ties down in Alabama?"

"Very same," Frank confirmed.

"Well, bless you, my boy," Bankhead chuckled, gesturing towards a chair. "Pull up a seat, and let's talk business, shall we?"

With the Senator's support, getting an appointment with Southern's Tie and Timber Agent, W. F. H. Fink, proved no big task. Now, the Southern Railroad building loomed over Frank like a stone titan, but he was undeterred. Steeling himself, Frank shouldered his bag and marched through the heavy oak doors. Inside, bureaucratic activity hummed, clerks scribbling on ledgers, typewriters clattering, and the hushed urgency of numbers and names and dates exchanged in whispers. He was right on time for his appointment, and hurried in.

The worn leather door of W.F.H. Fink's office creaked open, revealing a cramped space overflowing with papers and the imposing form of the Tie and Timber Agent himself. The stereotype of a railroad purchasing agent as a petty tyrant seemed to evaporate in Fink's presence. While undeniably powerful, with the authority to make or break a salesman's career, the man possessed an unexpected kindness. As Frank stood before the desk, feeling dwarfed by Fink's three-hundred-pound bulk, he was aware that the man was sizing him up. Perhaps it was Frank's youthful audacity or the glint in his eye, but Fink warmed quickly to the youth from Alabama.

"Well, son?" Fink smiled finally. "Let's see what you have to say."

For the next two hours, the office drowned in words and strategies. Frank, armed with meticulous calculations and a burning desire for success, parried Fink's every objection. He laid out his vision for a steady supply of high-quality crossties, delivered with unwavering efficiency. By the time the clock struck noon, Frank had secured the biggest crosstie contract the Southern Railroad had ever offered.

Leaving Fink's office, a heady mix of triumph and exhaustion coursed through Frank. He'd gambled on a trip to Washington, navigated the bureaucratic labyrinth, and emerged victorious. Returning to Calvert, a fire was ignited within him. "Well now, Frank, you're doin' it: *Operation Crosstie*," he declared to himself, the name rolling off his tongue with a sense of purpose.

It wasn't long before the once-quiet forests around Calvert echoed with the chop of axes and the groan of timber. Over seven hundred men, their calloused hands wielding saws and wedges, transformed the landscape. Days bled into nights as Frank pushed his crews to their limits. Fifty carloads of crossties became a regular occurrence. But he was no tyrant, no; Frank Boykin remained on the front line, and boundless energy was the lifeblood of the operation. He was a whirlwind of activity, overseeing logistics, securing financing, and even jumping in to help exhausted workers. Some days found him hauling a two-hundred-and-forty-pound crosstie, his body a testament to his own relentless spirit. They continued night and day, almost bow-legged from toting timber.

The timber might as well have been solid gold, because the financial rewards were tremendous. The Calvert store quickly transformed into a bustling, impromptu bazaar, sales skyrocketing with every passing week. Bacon, a staple for the hardworking Boykin crew, flew off the shelves faster than they could be restocked. Banks in Mobile, around 30 miles away, started bulging with Frank's ever-growing deposits. Meanwhile, in Malcolm, Alabama, his newfound wealth and vision coalesced in a two-story sawmill. A planing mill and a dry kiln, the first ever seen in Washington County, soon followed. Frank was building an empire, one fueled by hard work, shrewd business acumen, and an unwavering belief in his own potential.

But Frank hadn't forgotten the kindness of Senator Bankhead, who'd vouched for him when others might have scoffed. When election season rolled around, Frank jumped in feet first. With the same relentless energy that fueled his business ventures, he launched into a campaign unlike any Alabama had ever witnessed. His speeches, laced with his signature good humor and colorful personality, captivated audiences. Frank, the boy from Alabama, was fast becoming a political presence, and his skill and ability at lobbying was second to none.

The results, of course, were a landslide. Senator Bankhead, propelled by Frank's tireless campaigning, swept the county by a margin of five to one. It was a sweet victory, and it certified Frank's newfound influence and reputation as a good man to befriend. And as Frank surveyed his fledgling empire, all he could think was, *"Nowhere to go but up!"*

But again, things were never that simple.

***

Despite his success, things back at the store continued to be rough and tumble, and not everything was always smooth sailing.

By day, he ran the store with practiced efficiency, his booming voice keeping clerks on their toes and customers respectful. But nights, especially Saturdays, were a different story in this rough-and-tumble frontier town. Railroad men and lumberjacks, flush with wages and cheap whiskey, often turned the store into a rowdy saloon. Of course, Frank, a man built for trouble, wasn't easily intimidated. He kept his fists handy and his temper shorter. But even a good right hook couldn't always quell a man with a loaded pistol; that's why his twin pistols were more than just accessories. His sainted mother, a woman who otherwise wouldn't harm a fly, understood their necessity, and would make sure that he remembered them in the mornings when he would race to the store before the sun peeked over the horizon.

One time, it so happened that for three nights straight, the store had been broken into. Not a cent missing, not a bolt of cloth pilfered, just sidemeat—hams, shoulders, slabs of bacon—

vanished into the warm night. Frank, a man not known for patience when his livelihood was threatened, fumed.

On the fourth evening, after a day spent double-checking inventory, he oiled his pistols and made a decision. As the store settled into its usual nighttime quiet, Frank rigged the store for a nighttime stakeout. He stashed a blanket and some bread behind a counter for a long night's wait, strategically placed to offer both cover and a vantage point. Hours crawled by, and fatigue gnawed at his eyelids, but he remained alert.

Around two in the morning, a sound jolted him fully awake—a thump from the back window. In a flash, Frank was across the room. He crouched low and peering cautiously; he saw a hulking figure silhouetted against the moonlit night. A crowbar, glinting in the dark, pried open the window with a sickening groan. The figure, a tall black man, squeezed through the opening.

"You!" Frank roared, lunging from behind his flour barricade. The figure whirled around, startled, dropping the crowbar with a clatter. In the split second it took for recognition to register, a gunshot split the air. Frank had been shot in the left arm, sending him staggering back. The intruder capitalized; he snatched a side of bacon from a nearby shelf and scrambled back towards the window, hoisting himself through the opening before Frank could react. He landed with a splash in a waiting skiff bobbing on the dark waters of the Tombigbee River.

But Frank wasn't about to give up. Ignoring the pain in his arm, he sprinted toward the front of the store, still bleeding. Reaching the riverbank, he didn't hesitate; throwing caution to the wind, Frank dove into the chilly water. He ignored the throbbing pain in his arm, focusing on the silhouette of the fleeing thief. The current tugged at him, but Frank was a powerful swimmer, and he closed the distance steadily. Finally, he reached the thief's boat. Grappling onto the gunwale, he hauled himself in, sending the small vessel rocking precariously. The thief, a burly man with eyes wide with fear, scrambled to his feet.

The ensuing struggle was a blur of pain and exertion. The thief fought back with surprising ferocity. But Frank, a singularly tall and strong man, overpowered him and hauled the thief, panting and groaning, back towards the store. Half-carrying, half-dragging his prisoner as he still bled, Frank sent for the sheriffs.

For someone else, anyone else, this would have been one of the highlights of their life. For

Frank W. Boykin, this was just another footnote in a long and eventful life.

***

In time, the steel serpent of the railroad became Frank's personal travel agent. He saw it, then—fertile fields languishing, neglected by the locals, an opportunity ripe for the taking. These "chicken feed" parcels, as the saying went, were his oyster; he started small, a mere fifty dollars an acre for a plot bisected by a dirt road. It was his first bite of the apple, and it whetted his appetite. The AT&N railroad, sensing an opportunity, readily offered him a contract—a steady stream of income in exchange for a steady supply of firewood to fuel their iron steeds.

Fifty cents a cord. It wasn't a fortune, but it was reliable. Frank, ever resourceful, hired a crew of axemen—a ragtag bunch who transformed towering pines into bite-sized firebox lengths. The thud of axes intensified as the men felled the giants, hauling the chopped wood to be neatly stacked beside the tracks, within easy reach of the ravenous engines, and news of his land purchases spread like wildfire. Folks who'd spent years hawking their scraggly plots without a nibble suddenly saw Frank as a new tycoon in the making, albeit a self-made one, and they descended upon him like buzzards, eager to offload their unwanted acres for a pittance. It was a gold rush, fueled by their desperation and Frank's ambition.

One such offering struck a particularly personal chord. It was an old Boykin plantation, sold for a song years ago, its rich soil yearning for a new beginning. Frank knew what he had to do; he swooped in instantly, securing the return of the old plantation to the family fold for a measly dollar an acre. It was more than just an investment; it was a homecoming. At the same time, Frank had begun to understand the value of having a voice that was *heard,* and increasingly, he craved influence, a say in the shaping of his world.

But for now, Frank had a new project to devote all his time and effort to: an empire in the making.

Building an Empire

By the end of 1905, Frank Boykin stood at his twenty-first year with the beginnings of a complete fortune to his name—a milestone that, in most lives, prompted a moment of reflection. Indeed, he could have, if he chose, cashed in and walked away a millionaire. The Mobile banks held a hefty chunk of credit in his name—tangible proof of his great ambitions. Frank played the game like a high-stakes poker man, so confident in his hand he'd shove all his chips forward in a single, audacious move.

His career had been a classic rags-to-riches tale: a poor but honest boy, clawing his way up the ladder rung by rung, fueled by a potent blend of luck and sheer personality. One might even say the gods had bestowed upon him a Midas touch—anything he touched turned to gold, well, money at least. Despite his own limited education and barely eight months of formal schooling, Frank was fiercely determined to ensure his younger siblings wouldn't suffer the same fate. He shouldered the responsibility, seeing them through classrooms, even financing college for several. Family always came first to Frank, and he systematically drew his brothers and Boykin clan into his ever-expanding business ventures, increasing their holdings and solidifying their collective empire.

But Frank wasn't just accumulating inventory; he was stockpiling a different kind of wealth—intangible assets. His business sense, an uncanny knack honed by experience, not textbooks, thrummed through his veins. He had a gift for forging friendships, building a network as strong as any railroad crosstie he sold. And then there was his energy—boundless, relentless. A local reporter, years later, would quip that if Frank could be harnessed for power generation, he'd put the entire Tennessee Valley Authority and Alabama Power Company to shame. The powers-that-be had fashioned him with boundless energy—a man perpetually on the move, forever searching for the greener pastures just beyond the horizon. These same powers, perhaps out of a sense of fairness, had also blessed him with superhuman stamina and the uncanny ability to fall asleep anywhere, anytime. Fifteen minutes of slumber was all he needed to rise refreshed, prepared to break bread or prepare for war. This energy would then manifest in a whirlwind of rather manic activity, a blur of forestry deals, negotiations, and strategizing *the next big move.*

The next big move for Frank in the year 1906 was naval stores. It made sense: it was a field intimately linked to his timber operations, and with the confidence born of past successes, he dove in headfirst. Here, too, he embraced his motto: *never settle for small gains.* He added this new industry to his repertoire, though the transition wasn't seamless. Learning the intricacies of naval stores—the process of extracting turpentine, rosin, and other valuable products from pine trees—presented a fresh set of challenges. But Frank thrived on obstacles. Within months, his operation was humming, a well-oiled machine churning out profit alongside his timber business.

Frank continued to experiment with new techniques, constantly seeking an edge, a way to squeeze every ounce of value from the land. He challenged his crews, pushing them to think outside the box, and his drive was infectious. His workers, many from struggling families, saw in him a reflection of their own aspirations, and Frank was a familiar, jovial presence to many. They rallied behind him, and their combined efforts propelled his enterprises forward at a breakneck pace.

Frank had carved his own dominion in the region. The previous year, he had moved down to Malcolm, which, in 1905, was a small, rural community in Washington County, nestled in the southwest. The vast majority of the United States was still rural at this time, and Malcolm was no exception; it was a land of rolling hills, dotted with farms and woodlands. The primary industries were agriculture, with cotton being the dominant crop, and daily life revolved around this. Local travel still relied on dirt roads, and communication would have been limited. Mail reached Malcolm a few times a week, but telephones and widespread access to newspapers were still scarce.

His time was now split between Malcolm and the store in Calvert, between which the rhythmic clanging of the crosstie operation echoed through the woods, and the newly built dormitory hummed with the activity of his hired workers. The weathered trunks of lightwood Pine held hidden treasures for his naval store ambitions: pine oil, rosin, and turpentine. A fortune lay dormant within their woody fibers, a wealth just waiting to be extracted. Rosin and turpentine were the lifeblood of wooden ships, and Frank knew he wouldn't settle for being Alabama's biggest producer; he craved dominance.

The venture was sure to work, but Frank knew he needed a partner for this venture. His eye fell on John Everett, a seasoned Calvert resident, a man slightly older than Frank but full of quiet wisdom. John, a meticulous man with a keen eye for detail, was the perfect complement to Frank's go-getter spirit. Together, they formed Everett and Boykin, where Frank, as the natural frontman, would navigate the business world, securing deals and striking bargains. John, the steady hand behind the scenes, would ensure smooth operations, meticulous record-keeping, and efficient logistics.

The venture flourished from the start.

The pungency of pine filled the air as the distillation process chugged to life. Vats bubbled, releasing a heady concoction that was then meticulously separated into its constituent parts—golden rosin, clear turpentine, and potent pine oil. Each held immense commercial value, used in everything from paints and varnishes to medicines and cleaning products.

The life of an average turpentine worker in Frank's day was simple. Breakfast would be a quick affair—greasy bacon, fried mush, and strong coffee. The men would eat in silence, and words would be scarce before the day's labor began. They would then make their way to the towering pines and, using a brutal tool called a hack, would girdle a scrics of parallel cuts around the lower trunk of a pine. The white sap, rich with turpentine, would slowly bleed from these wounds. Days later, they'd return to collect it; they would then scoop the viscous liquid, which was emptied into a large metal bucket which, once full, would be hauled by a mule to a central collection point. By the time the foreman would end the day, the spent workers would have dinner, then a quick pipe under the star-dusted sky before collapsing back onto their mattresses. After a hard day's work, sleep would come easily.

Strong, rugged men such as these fueled Frank's ambitions and brought them to life. Under the watchful gaze of Spanish moss-draped oaks in Calvert, he erected a monument to his ambition—the largest turpentine distillery in the entire South. The price tag, a staggering sum whispered to be nearly a million dollars, sent shockwaves through the local gentry. Newspapers, starved for a juicy story, gushed about the engineering marvel, its defiant smokestack pointing towards the sky, and Frank, never one to shy away from the spotlight, basked in the newfound fame.

But Frank was looking for more—he was in it for the holy grail. As far as he was concerned, the traditional method of clearing land—grubbing out stubborn pine stumps by hand was too slow; Frank craved speed. In a move that had the old-timers shaking their heads, he brought in a new weapon: dynamite. The earth boomed with thunder as the once-immovable stumps were blasted from the ground, leaving behind a cratered moonscape. Dynamite salesmen, sniffing an opportunity, flocked to Frank like flies to honey, forever grateful for the audacious entrepreneur who'd made stump removal a booming business.

The success of Calvert spurred Frank on. Soon, turpentine plants sprouted like mushrooms across the landscape—in Malcolm, McIntosh, and Fairford. Each new day began the same way for Frank. Before the rooster even considered its crow, he'd be up, a pot of grits bubbling on the stove, a strong cup of coffee jolting him awake. His days were a whirlwind of inspections, his saddle as permanent a fixture as his boots. He rode one horse into the ground only to swap it for another, returning home, dust-caked and weary, just as the last sliver of sunlight dipped below the hungry horizon.

And the good news kept coming. Rosin prices, on a slow but steady climb, peaked at a dizzying twenty-six dollars a barrel. Frank's network of stills, ever insatiable, churned out a staggering fifteen hundred barrels a day, and every twenty-four hours, a crisp thirty-nine thousand dollars flowed into the coffers.

But there was a catch, of course. These stills were bottomless pits, and demanded more of the sticky, golden resin than was being harvested. Now, Frank had a setup that could handle far more production than it currently was, and he wasn't about to let that stay the case; thus began a new land acquisition spree. Thousands of acres—pine forests, riverfront plots, fertile tracts far upriver—all fell under his expanding empire. His ambition stretched south, crossing the invisible border into Baldwin County, a landmass larger than Rhode Island blessed with a soil capable of producing three crops a year. It turned out to be a goldmine.

"We could 'ave bought the whole damn county for a nickel-an-acre back then," Frank would later reminisce, shaking his head. "My only mistake was not buyin' more."

But Frank had succeeded in 1906 on more than the business front—he had also succeeded in realizing one of his most prized dreams, which was to allow his beloved parents to live a peaceable and worry-free live, with comforts bought from abundance that he had been blessed with. When Frank rose, the Boykins rose with him, and raised as he was in the south, Frank knew that family meant everything.

***

That June, the Alabama sun beat down mercilessly on Calvert. Inside Frank Boykin's general store, the air hung heavy with the scent of molasses, sawdust, and the smell of old books.

Just then, a tall figure, all angles, and sweat, pushed open the double swinging doors, momentarily disrupting the drowsy afternoon calm. Pushing forty with a lined but friendly face, the newcomer wore a coat despite the heat. Two bottles were stuck in his hip pockets.

"Well hello, I'm the proprietor," Frank said cheerfully, emerging from his office to shake the man's hand. "Glad to meet you! What can I do ya fer?"

"Name's Walter Bellingrath," the man replied, wiping sweat from his brow. "I'm the new bottlin' man down at Mobile for Coca-Cola."

Frank raised an eyebrow. "Never tasted the stuff."

Bellingrath shrugged, unfazed. "Well...you're about to," he declared, reaching into one of his hip pockets with a flourish to pick out one of the glass bottles. With a practiced flick of the wrist, Bellingrath popped the cap off and extended the bottle towards Frank.

Frank took a tentative sip. "Augh, that's terrible," he spluttered, wiping his mouth with the back of his hand. "Tastes like medicine or somesuch."

"Only because it's hot as blazes," Bellingrath laughed. "Stick it on ice, it'll be the best thing you ever put in your mouth. That's why I'm here—to see if you wouldn't mind carrying Coca-Cola in your stores. I'd like to send you a couple to try it out."

Coca-Cola, as Bellingrath explained, was a fledgling drink, popular in Georgia and Atlanta, but still unknown in most of Alabama. Frank knew well enough that soft drinks were all the rage nowadays, yet another fad at the turn of the century. Dozens of brands, each more garishly colored and mysteriously flavored than the last, competed for thirsty customers. Unfortunately, many also delivered a generous helping of stomach aches with their refreshment. Soda salesmen were as common as mosquitoes in the summer heat.

For this reason, Frank wasn't easily swayed. His shelves already groaned under the weight of four different soda brands. "Besides," he said, hoping to deflect the conversation, "how in tarnation did you get here?"

Bellingrath's grin widened. "Walked down the tracks from Malcolm."

Frank stared at him. "Great God! Ten-odd miles under this sun?"

"Saved ten cents," Bellingrath replied with a shrug.

In those days, freight trains offered a cheap, albeit unconventional, form of public transportation. A penny a mile for a short ride was a deal too good to pass up for traveling salesmen like Bellingrath. But it said something, Frank knew, of a man's dedication to walk ten miles in the Alabama heat to save a dime.

After a moment's contemplation, Frank had decided. "Tell you what," he said. "You send me ten cases of that Coca-Cola, freight prepaid. If it sells, you get your money right away. If not, I'll hop it back on the next train to Mobile."

Bellingrath nodded. "I'll agree to that," he said, shaking Frank's hand with enthusiasm. "But trust me, you won't be sending it back."

"Well, we'll see what we'll see," Frank chuckled. "Now, how about some lunch? It's past time, and the next train south isn't leaving for a good hour."

Perhaps, Frank thought, watching Bellingrath devour a hefty sandwich, this new fizzy concoction might just be the next big thing. It was time to find out.

Two days later, Frank found himself looking at ten cases of Coca-Cola sitting at the Calvert AT&N station. On one hand, ice was a precious commodity in Calvert; the nearest ice plant was in Mobile, miles away, and deliveries were scarce. Then it occurred to him; behind his store stood an old, forgotten well, known for its refreshingly cold water. He called upon his long-time porter, Tom Armistead.

"Tom," Frank declared, "I need me an old tub. Put it by the well and fill it with these here Coca-Cola bottles. Then, draw enough water from the well to submerge 'em completely." Frank paused, visualizing his plan. "Then, every hour, on the hour, mind you, refill the tub with fresh well water. Let it sit for five cycles, then move it in the store."

The plan was simple, yet ingenious. The cool well water would act as a makeshift refrigerator, chilling the Coca-Cola to a temperature enticing to the heat-weary customer. And Frank's gamble paid off; the ten cases sold out within the first day, snapped up by thirsty patrons eager for a taste of the cool beverage. Seeing this success, Frank wasted no time and immediately re-ordered ten cases, then another ten for each of his other stores. Soon, he became Bellingrath's biggest customer along the Tombigbee River.

Taking Chances

Later that year, Frank Boykin and John Everett arrived at Baldwin County.

Back in 1906, Baldwin County spread out along the eastern shore of Mobile Bay, surrounded landwards by dense green cathedrals of towering pines, punctuated by the occasional, gnarled live oak. Sunlight, filtered through the verdant canopy, would dapple the forest floor in a church mosaic, and there was no mistake: this place of surpassing beauty was undeniably a land of ripe and ample opportunity. All who saw this verdant stretch could not help but be moved.

This shoreline, a sinuous ribbon of white sand that locals called "America's Riviera," was where the wilderness met the embrace of the bay. Dotted with charming towns boasting names like Daphne, Fairhope, and Montrose, the coast held a hint of forgotten elegance. In bygone eras, the wealthy elite of Mobile, weary of the city's clamor, had built grand summer homes here, seeking solace in the sylvan delights of Baldwin County. Generations of pleasure-seekers had flocked to Point Clear, the crown jewel of the coastline, its white sand beach a playground for the privileged.

But Everett and Boykin weren't drawn to Baldwin County for its captivating beauty or its luxurious retreats. Their sights were set on the vast tracts of virgin pine forests that stretched around Point Clear and Grand Bay, the shapely arm of Mobile Bay. Fueled by the insatiable demand for naval stores, they embarked on an aggressive land acquisition campaign, leasing or buying thousands of acres. Their mission wasn't to revel in the county's natural wonders; it was to exploit them. Their aim was to "cup" the pines on a grand scale, a process akin to how Vermont maple farmers tapped sugar maples. Here, however, the target wasn't sweet sap, but sticky, golden resin—the lifeblood of the turpentine industry. Crews of men, armed with axes and driven by efficient timetables, would hack into the trunks of the towering pines, creating deep, V-shaped wounds. Over a million of these gashes, like gaping mouths, would ooze the precious resin, a viscous amber liquid destined to be distilled into turpentine and rosin, essential ingredients in a multitude of products.

The forests now began to work for Boykin's ambition, and trails carved through the undergrowth became arteries filtered by an ever-expanding network of crude collecting stations that were scattered across the vast expanse. Here, the sticky resin, thick as molasses, was channeled into wooden buckets, its journey far from over. From these temporary outposts, it would be carted by mule-drawn wagons to waiting barges on the Mobile & Tensaw River Railroad, a vital artery that snaked its way through the county, carrying the lifeblood of the industry to the waiting maw of the stills.

That Thanksgiving, surrounded as he was by duty and the business of maintaining the industry in Baldwin County, he was unable to spend the evening with his family. For a man brought up on traditional family values, this rankled in Frank Boykin's heart, and so he resolved to write his mother a letter. Sitting down on a heavy oak table covered with paperwork, he began to write:

My Dear, Dear Mama,

I'm so sorry I can't be with you all today, but I've thought of all of you more than once, thought of how very many things we everyone had to be thankful for today and I am thankful, and above all things I'm thankful for one of the sweetest, dearest Mothers that ever lived...

But his hard work was paying off—with interest. As their business flourished, the Everett-Boykin partnership became synonymous with burgeoning prosperity. Frank had also realized that the land they'd acquired for the turpentine operation, stretching across vast swathes of Alabama and dipping into the fertile crescent of Baldwin County, presented a new opportunity. "Real estate," declared Frank, his eyes gleaming with a familiar glint. Everett, ever the voice of reason, raised an eyebrow, but Frank was already a whirlwind of ideas. Together, they opened a real estate business that took off like a rocket. Their slogan, "We enjoy the thrill of selling land by the square mile," was a testament to their infectious enthusiasm. One successful development followed another, each one a testament to their vision, slowly but surely expanding the city's boundaries. Frank, ever the showman, took to boasting that only Napoleon, with his Louisiana Purchase, could rival the sheer expanse of land they'd brought under their wing.

As far as Frank was concerned, they were destined to be in every business that could possibly turn a profit.

One such venture, fueled by Frank's boundless optimism, was satsuma oranges. Baldwin County's rich soil, bathed in year-round sunshine, seemed like the perfect cradle for these sweet citrus fruits. Everett and Boykin, never ones to do things halfway, began planting with a fervor that bordered on obsession; row upon row of citrus trees stretched as far as the eye could see, transforming vast tracts of land into a checkerboard of green leaves and golden fruit. Come fall, the oranges, heavy with juice, hung like miniature suns. The sight was breathtaking, and a photographer hired by Frank captured it all on film—rolling hills bursting with sunshine-kissed oranges, ready to be shipped north by the trainload.

For a while, their citric empire flourished. The trains rumbled north, laden with the sweet citrus bounty, bringing in a steady stream of revenue. But fate, it seemed, had a particularly wicked sense of humor. One particularly harsh winter, a frost descended upon Baldwin County, a silent thief stealing the lifeblood from their orange groves. Now, these trees stood bare and skeletal; their once vibrant green leaves transformed into a drab, lifeless brown. This unexpected turn of events left the partners grappling with the extensive damage to the valuable citrus crops; in a fell stroke, the bounty of plenty had turned into a desolate graveyard.

The Satsuma fiasco nearly broke them, but John Everett and Frank Boykin were made of sterner stuff. Where other men would pack up shop and play it safe, they rolled up their sleeves and kept going.

Part II

The Interim

(1906 - 1934)

Winds of Fortune

By 1906, Frank and John controlled a vast domain stretching from Mobile to McIntosh, a forty-mile swathe of land tamed by calloused hands and the relentless tug of oxen in the deep woods. And so, the duo had made a decision—by year's end, they would dissolve their partnership, selling their assets and dividing the proceeds. Retirement beckoned for both, and their futures lay on separate paths.

And Frank now got back to work. The railroad coughed and wheezed, hauling logs to the sawmills, and all seemed well. But the drudgery, in time, began to feel like a worn harness. He craved a taste of something finer; fishing expeditions, thrilling hunts, soirees—these were the visions that danced in his head, a life inspired to be spent in the pursuit of happiness, as Thomas Jefferson would put it. And though work was never far from his mind, Frank Boykin decided to pause for a moment and smell the roses.

Thus, the Carlotta arrived, Frank Boykin's prized yacht. A vision in polished wood and gleaming brass, she glided into Mobile Bay with the grace of a swan. Compared to the leviathans owned by the Northern elite, she was a mere minnow. Yet, in Mobile, she was a revolution. Crowds thronged the docks, marveling at her sleek lines and the promise of extravagance she embodied.

He stocked her with the finest provisions – aged bourbon, French champagne that tickled the tongue, and the finest cigars. A flotilla of friends, chosen for their appreciation of a good time, were assembled. The route was a loose promise: wanderlust as their compass. They dreamt of lazy days punctuated by fishing trips and evenings filled with laughter and the clinking of glasses. They weren't sure exactly where they were going, but they certainly knew they were going to have a good time.

Fate, however, seemed to have other plans.

On the 7th of September, 1906, it arrived with a sinister whisper on the southern horizon—a lone cloud, no larger than a clenched fist, drifted into view. It grew, morphing into a hulking beast, its belly churning with a darkness that promised destruction. Within the hour, the winds descended upon Mobile like a pack of ravenous wolves. They shrieked and howled, tearing at windows and whipping the placid bay into a frenzy. The sky dissolved into an inkwell, unleashing an unrelenting torrent of rain. The once gentle bay, a golden reflection of the sun, transformed into a raging monster. Egged on by an eighty-mile-per-hour hurricane, it rose like a tidal wave, pushing a wall of water that crested the embankment and surged into the city. Rivers, overwhelmed by the deluge, turned renegade, flooding the land for miles. Streets bordering the bay became watery highways, swallowing anything in their path. The hurricane, a ruthless sculptor, ripped into the city. Ancient oaks that had weathered centuries of storms were uprooted and flung about like toys. Houses bore the brunt of their fury, splintering and collapsing under the onslaught.

And as Frank watched from the shore, his beloved Carlotta was tossed by the storm. A monstrous wave, a leviathan carved from churning water, lifted the yacht from her anchorage. He witnessed, with a horrifying detachment, as she pirouetted in the air before being unceremoniously deposited on the roof of the Southern Railroad's nearby freight house. The sun, when it finally fought its way through the tattered clouds, revealed a scene of devastation. The roundhouse of the Louisville & Nashville railroad stood submerged, a graveyard of locomotives, their fires extinguished by the storm's fury. Up north, Frank's timber kingdom lay in ruins. Sawmills were reduced to a tangled mess of wood and debris. His turpentine stills, once humming with activity, lay crumpled on the sodden earth. The wind, a thief in the night, had snatched away countless barrels of the precious liquid, dashing them to the ground like broken toys. Even his commissary stores felt the scars of the storm.

The storm had ripped through his dreams; but resolutely, Frank refused to surrender. He, like the mighty pines that had withstood countless storms before, would rebuild.

With a fervor born of desperation, Frank threw himself into the task of resurrecting his fortune. Sawmills hummed back to life, their blades eager to devour the fallen giants. But triumph soon turned to despair. The first log, hauled up the ramp with the optimism of a new beginning, revealed a devastating truth. The storm's fury had not merely felled the trees; it had twisted them, contorted them into useless spirals. Imagine, Frank must have thought, a man twisting a rope – that's how the storm had ravaged his precious timber. Saws bit into the warped wood, but the resulting boards were destined to crumble into splinters. These twisted logs held no value.

Yet, even in the face of such crushing disappointment, Frank refused to succumb, continuing to work with a sense of tempered optimism. Though his luck began to shift, he remained cautious now, having learned from the past. The New Year dawned, and with it came a renewed sense of national optimism. From the opalescent walls of the White House, the energetic and boisterous new President of the United States of America, Theodore Roosevelt, ushered in a new era in American politics, living a personal life of hard work, adventure, and engagement. Under these auspices, 1907 promised boundless fortune, but while "experts" in Washington gazed into their crystal balls and prophesied perpetual prosperity, Frank harbored a healthy dose of skepticism. He knew by now that every ascent carried the inevitable descent, even if it were just a partial retreat.

This knowledge, however, did not breed pessimism. Instead, it fueled a cautious optimism. Frank understood that the economic future, much like the weather, could shift dramatically. He would prepare for the sunshine, but also keep a watchful eye on the gathering storm clouds.

But the nation, oblivious to the potential dangers lurking on the horizon, sailed full steam ahead into the New Year, blissfully unaware of the coming economic tempest. By now, the American landscape was dominated by the rise of colossal Trusts and ruthless business combinations that squeezed out smaller competitors with ruthless efficiency. These "malefactors of great wealth," as Roosevelt famously dubbed them, controlled vast swathes of industry – meat, bread, coal, steel – and operated with an iron fist. Labor unrest grew louder, a simmering pot threatening to boil over as workers grappled with harsh conditions and stagnant wages in the face of immense corporate profits. From the pulpit of the White House, Roosevelt thundered against these Trusts, but his efforts did not bear fruit.

Then, the year took a sharp turn in the middle when a financial panic swept across the nation like a hurricane. Businesses sputtered, credit tightened, and the once-reliable engines of progress, like the railroads, slowed to a crawl. This turmoil reached Frank's doorstep in Mobile, Alabama, where the substantial savings of the now defunct Everett-Boykin partnership were still jointly held in the People's Bank. As news broke that the bank was on shaky ground, Frank rushed to withdraw the money. But there, he was met by a desperate plea from the bank president, one Alfred Staples, who implored him not to break the bank by pulling out their funds.

"Frank, don't you be takin' your money out!" Staples said as he leaned forward earnestly, his shirt unironed. "Y'know that would go and break the bank if you do, see?"

Sighing, Frank agreed to a compromise: he withdrew only a fraction of the savings, ten thousand dollars, just enough to provide a safety net in uncertain times. Thankfully, the People's Bank, though teetering, did not collapse. It was eventually absorbed by a stronger institution, and Frank and John Everett's money, along with that of other depositors, was eventually repaid.

**

In time, Frank succeeded in his efforts to rebuild, and Turpentine stills again dominated the Southern landscape, churning out enough rosin to make Frank the undisputed kingpin of the industry, not just in Alabama, but quite possibly the entire nation. These assets from the old Everett-Boykin partnership still sat, and though everyone had expected them to be sold soon after the duo dissolved their partnership, Frank bided his time. It was only in 1909 when, with his uncanny knack for sniffing out the perfect moment, Frank made a decision: he was selling. Lock, stock, and barrel, the entire turpentine operation was going to a group of tight-lipped bankers from New York. The price was astronomical, high enough to choke a mule.

1912 rolled around without great incident. Frank Boykin remained enamored with the land; he saw its potential and its ability to generate wealth, and he craved it. Unlike many in the post-Civil War South who viewed landownership as stagnant, Frank saw an opportunity. His ambition, coupled with his relentless work ethic, became his recipe for success. He believed in hard work and wasn't afraid of a fight.

One such fight involved an 8,600-acre tract near Mobile, Alabama. The land, once the hunting ground of the Chickasaw tribe, was ideally situated—close to the city and with significant riverfrontage. Frank envisioned a future bustling with industry on this land. But the owner, a stubborn old codger named Colonel Burgess, clung to the property like a lifeline. Frustrated by failed attempts to buy the land through intermediaries, Frank took matters into his own hands. He raced to

New York City, determined to outmaneuver Burgess's son-in-law who was also on his way to block the sale.

Frank found Burgess at a hotel bar and launched straight into his pitch. Burgess, initially resistant, softened as Frank painted a vibrant picture of Mobile's future, a future that hinged on the Colonel selling this very piece of land. The conversation stretched through the afternoon, punctuated by meals and Frank's witty stories.

By 2 am, Burgess was exhausted but surprisingly willing to negotiate. He named his price--$25 an acre, all cash upfront. This presented a major hurdle. Frank's bank balance wouldn't even cover half the $215,000 cost. Sleepless but determined, he worked through the night. Frantic calls were made. Banks were approached, and a loan was secured from a friendly banker who remembered a past favor. By morning, Frank had miraculously scraped together the necessary funds.

Unbeknownst to him at the time, though, a stroke of luck had intervened; Burgess, basking in the glory of the deal, had wasted the day showing off the check, delaying its arrival at the bank. This precious extra day gave Frank the time he needed to get the money in place, and now the deal was sealed: Frank had secured a magnificent piece of land, a future industrial hub, for a steal. As far as he was concerned, God had taken the reigns—though there's also no denying the power of his ambition.

Now, Frank once again was free to continue his 'pursuit of happiness'. Like Roosevelt, who he admired, Frank Boykin was drawn to the wilderness like a moth to the flame. Just as Roosevelt yearned for the rugged peaks of the Rockies in pursuit of mountain sheep, Boykin felt a similar pull towards the wilds; the very essence of the hunt held a magnetic charm for him. The hunt wasn't just about acquiring a trophy; it was an adventure, a test of skill in the face of the unknown. There are to this day photos of him in hunting grounds, surrounded by breathtaking landscapes and impressive trophies, living in pursuit of a "strenuous life", as Roosevelt liked to call it.

But hunting and business weren't his only great distractions. The pursuit of game and wealth left ample room for romance, and Frank had mastered the Boykin charm. Every small town along the Tombigbee had girls whose hearts fluttered at the sight of Frank Boykin; a mere cheery "halloo" as the train whisked him away would be enough to be taken by this lively, cheerful man. Perhaps it was his preordained magnetism, the sparkle in his eyes that danced with mischief and ambition—or perhaps it was his generosity, his penchant for spoiling the ladies with luxurious gifts.

He wielded his rich, Southern charisma with the finesse of a maestro, disarming women with casual familiarity. There was, for instance, the legendary encounter with Miss America, courtesy of Arkansas's own Representative Brooks Hays. Frank, the ever-effusive charmer, gave her his best smile and smoothly noted, "Honey, you're so beautiful you *couldn'ta* come from Arkansas. No sir, you must have come straight down from 'eaven."

This very year, the White House and the political landscape of the country churned as Woodrow Wilson's presidential win became a national headline. But for Frank, who had just closed one of the greatest deals of his life and was too busy spending time with the gals, the dusty world of politics held little sway. Yet as he laughed, celebrated, and charmed his days away, little did he know that this was the year when he would fall, utterly and totally, in love.

A Man in Love

The whistle of the approaching train shattered the stillness of the morning, as grimy tracks snaked their way towards a lone wooden depot. Here, the train Frank awaited would soon groan to a halt, near the camp where rough-hewn wooden shacks huddled together in the dew-damp earth. Smoke curled from chimneys, carrying the pungent aroma of pine sap and simmering resin, as the air vibrated with the rhythmic clang of an unseen axe. The sweet, almost sickening, scent of pine sap hung heavy, mingling with the acrid smoke and the earthy dampness of the forest floor—but it was a smell Frank was used to, and he barely noticed it in his excitement as he dismounted from his horse.

Today was the day.

Today, he'd meet the woman who'd set tongues wagging across the county: one Miss Ocllo Gunn. He had heard of her beauty and, finally, decided to investigate for himself as to who this lady was.

From what he knew, Ocllo Gunn, with her brunette tresses, was in stark contrast to her ancestors, who had once been of Viking stock. The Gunn family history began with the blue-eyed and fair-haired Norse raiders that had centuries ago settled in Scotland, their legacy preserved in the family crest—a Viking longship, sails billowing, oars churning, and a hand brandishing a sword above it. The motto, "Aut Pax Aut Bellum," declared "Either Peace or War."

This spirit of fierce independence was apparent in Ocllo's willful choice to become a teacher despite having no immediate need to do so. Yet her lineage was also intertwined with education; her great-grandfather, John Greene, had established Alabama's first school the year before the state joined the Union. John, with a name befitting a pioneer, bestowed the unusual name "Ocllo" on his daughter, inspired by Parkman's history of the Incas. The name had carried on in the family, carrying within it the legacy of a strong, faraway princess. And so Ocllo Gunn was a woman carrying the legacy of two worlds—the Old World and the New.

Graduating with a degree in English literature in 1909, Ocllo wasn't one to chase wealth or fame. Ambition for a career in education fueled her, and she landed a teaching job in Fulton, Alabama, with no means to marry into wealth whatsoever.

But destiny had other plans.

Word had reached Frank that the lady he longed to meet would be taking the southbound rail to a party at McIntosh in the home of Frank's cousin. About midday, Ocllo's train would pass his turpentine camp below Jackson and pause there to pick up passengers. Now, his plan was to face her at exactly this moment. Armed with nothing but a gambler's bravado, Frank waited beside the dusty tracks, his gaze fixed on the plume of smoke rising in the distance. Descriptions of Ocllo's beauty had painted vivid pictures in his mind, and he was curious whether the damsel in his mind matched the one upon whom he was about to lay his eyes.

The screech of metal shattered the quiet, but the iron serpent did not lumber to a halt; spewing a cloud of steam, it continued to run as the conductor saw no reason to stop for a single figure on the platform. Frank's pulse quickened as he scrambled to retrieve his horse. Mounted, he charged beside the train, looking from window to window, until—there, there she was, unmistakable even from afar, a vision, her brunette hair cascading down. Three young women, all impeccably dressed, accompanied her. Frank's carefully rehearsed introduction evaporated—she more than matched up to his imagination. Now, nerves clawed at his throat, leaving him momentarily speechless as she looked at him in astonishment.

Then, with characteristic boldness, his voice booming above the chug of the train and the desperate gallop of his steed, he announced: *"Miss Gunn, I presume! I'm Frank Boykin...an' I intend on marryin' you someday!"*

The effect was instantaneous. Ocllo's eyes widened even further in surprise, a flush creeping up her cheeks. The other women exchanged bewildered glances, momentarily speechless at this audacious intrusion.

Before Ocllo could utter a word, the conductor's whistle rang out as the train picked pace. With a showman's grin, Frank threw one last, hopeful look at Ocllo, whose face was a mixture of amusement and disbelief, then turned and mirrored an exit worthy of the knights of old, cantering away gracefully. Riding back to the turpentine camp, his heart thumped a victory march. He may have startled the lovely Miss Ocllo, but he had certainly made an impression. And for a man like Frank Boykin, that was just the beginning. The chase for the hand of Ocllo Gunn had begun, and Frank intended to win.

The audacity of Frank Boykin's declaration echoed through Thomasville like a clap of thunder. The gossip mill churned, turning his train-chasing proclamation into a legend—audacious, unconventional, possibly even scandalous. Miss Ocllo, the object of his sudden affection, found herself the unwilling heroine in a whirlwind romance she hadn't signed up for. At first, the public declaration felt intrusive, and a spotlight suddenly cast on her private life. Yet, a flicker of something else stirred within her—a spark of intrigue. The sheer boldness of it all, the unbridled confidence of this man she barely knew, piqued her curiosity.

Her parents, however, were not impressed. Mr. and Mrs. Gunn, pillars of Thomasville society, clung to a more traditional courtship. Frank's unorthodox approach felt like an outsider breaching the castle walls. To make matters worse, the rumors that followed him, whispers of fleeting dalliances in other towns, only fueled their disapproval. Their daughter, their precious Ocllo, deserved a steady suitor.

Frank, however, wasn't one to give up easily. Undeterred by the initial rejection, he launched a full-court press. Telephones buzzed with his calls, telegrams arrived daily, and his letters, penned in a flamboyant script that mirrored his personality, flooded Ocllo's room. The sheer volume of his affections was overwhelming.

Ocllo, caught between the whirlwind of Frank's advances and the disapproval of her parents, found herself in a precarious position. A part of her, the rebellious streak she barely acknowledged, found a certain amusement in Frank's antics. He was a stark contrast to the gentlemanly suitors her parents would have preferred, all bland smiles and predictable conversations. Frank was a force of nature, unpredictable and passionate, a whirlwind in a starched collar. Yet, the voice of reason, nurtured by her upbringing, echoed her parents' concerns. Was his ardor genuine, or simply a fleeting fancy? Could a future built on such a hasty foundation be stable? She found herself poring over his letters, searching for clues beneath the flowery language and passionate declarations, but the conflict within her remained unresolved. Her head cautioned against haste, urging her to wait for a more traditional, predictable suitor. Yet, her heart, stirred by the sheer audacity of it all, couldn't ignore the spark ignited by Frank's bravado.

This indecision and her parents' opposition to the courtship was beginning to show Frank that an alternative approach was needed. As he paced in his office like a caged panther, he decided that he needed to meet Ocllo's mother face to face, convinced that once he charmed her, the path to Ocllo's heart would be smoother. But Mrs. Gunn remained a formidable obstacle, a gatekeeper unwilling to give him an audience. His letters to Ocllo overflowed with this frustration, tinged with a touch of wounded pride.

I want to ask you one thing: are you going to let what other people say, people that don't know me, haven't ever seen me, keep you from letting me come to see you? I bet I can come to see any other girl in Thomasville and there won't be a word said. It's funny to me that I can go with the best, the very best girls in Mobile, Birmingham, Memphis, New Orleans or, for that matter, any other little or big town I've been in. It's strange to me that it's such a disgrace for me to come to see you, I don't see how it is ruining your life, and more than that, I don't see to save my life where it is anybody else's business.

His words resonated with Ocllo. While tradition dictated a more formal courtship, a small voice inside her rebelled at the thought of letting others dictate her happiness. Yet, she couldn't ignore her mother's concerns. Frank's reputation, deserved or not, cast a long shadow.

So for a while, Frank suffered a long silence. But one afternoon, a ray of hope arrived in the form of a note from Ocllo. Her mother, it seemed, was planning a trip to Mobile, taking the southbound train that stopped briefly at Calvert down the line. In the letter, Ocllo veiled a suggestion—that he do as he felt best.

Frank was overjoyed: here was his chance. On the appointed day, he waited impatiently at the Calvert station, where the sun-bleached wooden walls offered meager protection from the scalding southern sun. Every once in a while, he would squint at the dusty timetable that adorned the wall, detailing the arrival and departure times of the southbound and northbound trains, a bouquet of lilies clutched nervously in his hand. In time, the train rolled in, releasing a plume of steam as it shuddered to a halt. Passengers disembarked, a blur of faces until his gaze landed on a woman with a dignified air, unmistakably Ocllo's mother.

It was the time for the performance of his life. Taking a deep breath, he approached her with a warm smile and launched into his carefully rehearsed speech. He spoke of his intentions, his respect for Ocllo, and his unwavering love as he poured out his charm, his business acumen transformed into promises and aspirations. Mrs. Gunn, initially skeptical and in a hurry, gradually found herself drawn into his whirlwind of emotions. Before she fully realized it, she had succumbed to his relentless but sincere appeal; he would be allowed to call on Ocllo, but only after her return to Thomasville. It was not surrender, but it was a concession nonetheless—and Frank, overjoyed, embraced it wholeheartedly.

His jubilation poured out in a letter to Ocllo, a love letter laced with breathless excitement. "Ocllo, darling," he wrote, "I simply fell in love with her. I really and truly enjoyed every minute I was with her... I am invited to come to Thomasville whenever I wish. Darn it! I've been ready for months!"

The news spread quickly through Thomasville, creating a buzz of anticipation. Ocllo, still a little hesitant, found herself caught in the tide of change. Her parents, while not fully convinced, tacitly agreed to the new arrangement. Frank, no longer the unwelcome suitor, was now a welcomed guest, albeit one under careful scrutiny. Their courtship blossomed under the watchful eye of Mrs. Gunn. Frank, ever eager to please, showered them both with attention. He presented Ocllo with elaborate gifts, from imported French perfume to custom-made riding boots. He charmed Mrs. Gunn with tales of his business ventures, his genuine warmth softening her initial reservations.

All was going well, and as 1913 approached, the love in Frank Boykin's heart grew. He had long since arrived mentally at the idea that everything was indeed made for love, and the past summer and winter of his blissful contentment had only strengthened this idea. As Spring now bloomed across Alabama, love bloomed in Frank's heart. Come May Day, in a letter overflowing with endearment, he poured his soul out to Ocllo. "My Own Darling..." he began, his words laced with a passionate desperation.

My Own Darling:

Honey, I wonder if you will ever know how much, how very much I love you. Ocllo, I love you madly, I am just wild to hold you in my arms, to look into those eyes I love so dearly and kiss you most breathless. It is so good to have somebody to love and just look who I am loving! You're just what I've always needed. I just have to come and get you. Ocllo, I can't do without you. It's awful to have to be separated. Ocllo, for goodness' sake write me when I can come.

I love you so, darling, I love, love, love you. I love you, darling, and nobody else but you.

I could write a million pages.

Always forever,

Your Frank.

A few days later, still basking in the afterglow of his emotions, Frank boarded a train to Mobile. His destination? A jeweler's on Bienville Square. Land, the lifeblood of his business, might have echoed in his thoughts constantly, but love, for the moment, took precedence. He intended now to purchase a ring for his beloved Ocllo.

The ring he chose was extravagant and far from cheap. A pang of guilt flickered within him—this money, after all, could have been used to expand his empire, to buy more land, thus further securing his future with his beloved wife-to-be. Yet, the desire to see it adorn Ocllo's finger outweighed his practical concerns for a moment. Love, it seemed, had a way of bending even the most pragmatic of minds—but on his return journey, fate intervened in the form of A.M. Wing, an old friend. The conversation flowed easily, and amidst the camaraderie, Wing suddenly spoke up.

"Frank, I want to get married. But see, I need me a ring, and I haven't got myself enough money to buy one," Wing said, bemoaning his circumstances.

"Well, truth be told, I'm gettin' married myself. I just bought me a pro-per diamond ring." Frank chimed, still riding the high of his own love-induced euphoria as proudly displayed the recently purchased diamond. Wing's envious whistle echoed through the train car. "I'm goin' to be givin' this ol' stone to my Ocllo on Saturday night."

"Whew!" Wind said. "It's a bona-fide beauty, that! Wish I could buy me one just like it."

Ever the opportunist, Frank gazed at the diamond as if suddenly entranced—he had an idea. But...what would Ocllo say? Ultimately, the allure of a good deal proved too strong to resist. He broached a proposition.

"Well..." said Frank slowly, "What'd you take for your plantation 'ere on the Tombigbee?"

"Frank...you give me that ring and several-hundred square dollars to boot, and *it's a deal*," Wing blurted out. "Listen, I've got twenty-three hundred good, ripe acres in the property. It's good land, Frank. What d'ya say?"

Frank agreed gustily, and a deal was struck—a wedding ring and some spare, traded for 2300 acres of fertile land. The wedding itself would now be delayed until Frank could buy another ring. Ocllo, though initially displeased by the delay, understood the logic behind Frank's impulsive decision. After all, love could wait; a potential goldmine couldn't. And indeed, her patience bore fruit as well—off that plantation, Frank cut over a hundred thousand dollars worth of timber, trading hunting rights to stay ahead of the taxes. Full of game, deer, wild turkey, and even bear, the property was bountiful and would help the Boykin fortunes advance ever further.

Finally, after having enough for a second ring, it was time. It was December 31st, 1913, and the year was drawing to a close with a joyous occasion: the wedding of Frank Boykin and Ocllo Gunn in the First Baptist Church in Thomasville. Bathed in the soft glow of winter sunlight filtering through the narrow windows, a whirlwind courtship came to a happy conclusion. As the ceremony concluded, cheers and congratulations erupted, washing over the newly married couple.

Later, amidst the flurry of well-wishes and celebratory toasts, Frank presented Ocllo with his wedding gift to her: a magnificent black saddle horse named Diamond, its midnight coat gleaming like polished obsidian under the soft light. To make up for his deal and the delay, Frank had given Ocllo two diamonds—one in her ring, and one in the shape of the handsome horse that reminded her of the day Frank Boykin, like a modern-day knight gallant, had galloped alongside a train to declare his love.

Fire, Friends, and Fortune

The years span as history spins, and the wheel of time landed on 1917. The world was churning with the chaos of war, the Great War, as they called it—the war to end all wars, as it was called, in a spirit of desperate optimism. Tensions in Europe had crackled like a lit fuse since the summer of 1914. The assassination of the heir to the Austro-Hungarian throne by a Serbian nationalist on June 28th had kicked off a chain reaction, triggering a domino effect of alliances. Within a week, a localized conflict in the Balkans had morphed into a full-blown global war, and the continent sleepwalked into a catastrophe that would reshape the world for decades to come.

As Europe burned, an ocean away, the American public grappled with a complex mix of emotions—a sense of detachment, a growing unease, and simmering patriotism.

Initially, the war felt distant. News traveled by telegram and steamship, painting a blurry picture of trench warfare and gas attacks. Headlines screamed of battles with unfamiliar names—Verdun, Somme, Ypres—far removed from the cornfields of Iowa or the bustling streets of New York. Many Americans felt a sense of neutrality. "Why should we get involved in a European squabble?" was a common refrain.

However, neutrality became increasingly difficult to maintain. German U-boats and submarines sank American ships, killing innocent civilians. The infamous sinking of the Lusitania in 1915, with over 1200 lives lost, ignited a wave of anger. Parades and rallies in favor of intervention became commonplace. Even the pacifists found their voices drowned out by the growing chorus of war cries. In this very year, President Wilson finally grew convinced that American intervention was necessary to make the world safe for democracy. Meanwhile, the war in Europe also brought fortune to America. Factories, managed by shrewd hands of the business, had shifted production to meet the demands of the Allies, Britain, France, and Russia. This remarkably foresighted pivot brought economic prosperity, with jobs plentiful and wages rising.

Indeed, one of the Boykins even fought in the trenches on the Maginot Line in France in the Great War. But when Marvin 'Buck' Boykin returned home, he was suffering from 'Shell Shock', what is now understood to be PTSD. Due to this, he was unable to work or raise his daughters Helen and Glo. Frank was devastated and supported Buck for the rest of his life—a fact that I, the author, can personally attest to. For you see, Helen is the name of this author's mother, and Buck Boykin was none other than my own grandfather.

***

Back in Frank's ever-bustling drugstore, a familiar black soda dominated the shelves, and the Boykin share in the coke-craze was beginning to pay for itself. Coca-Cola sales had soared amidst wartime, its sweet, caffeinated comfort a welcome distraction for a world on edge.

By now, his longtime trade partner, Walter Bellingrath, was a married man, and Frank got to know the Bellingraths well from the early days of their joint venture—decent, hard-working folks who seemed to scrape by on sheer grit. When they first met, the Bellingrath's modest financial condition was evident; indeed, Walter's loose suit had seemed to hang off his lanky frame. Yet, even then, their personalities shone brightly. Walter's eyes held an air of open honesty, and Bessie's smile radiated a warmth akin to the southern sun; Frank, always a good judge of character, knew that these were good folk, and he made a point to associate well enough with them. Their status did not much matter to him, but he knew that prosperity comes to all those deserving, and the Bellingraths were certainly deserving.

Fast forward a few years, and Frank's hunch proved right. Walter had become a man of fortune... a fair amount of it. Coca-Cola, that magical elixir, had fueled his ascent, nickel by nickel—enough nickels, in fact, to build a quaint fishing cottage nestled down by the bayou on Fowl River, a place soon to be known as Isle-aux-Oies—Goose Island.

Fowl River, a mere 14.4 miles long, snaked its way from near Theodore, splitting into a graceful braid—the East Fowl and West Fowl. The river wasn't particularly deep, averaging less than ten feet, but within its shallow heart, a rich ecosystem pulsed. Bald eagles soared overhead, their cries echoing across the water. Ospreys perched on branches, and alligators basked on muddy banks. Once, the famed Irish pirate, Paddy Scott, had used its hidden paths to slip in and out unseen, and this romantic, beautiful waterway had been a long part of the grand drama that unfolded along the Alabama coast.

Crouched upon this rich river, Isle-aux-Oies became a haven for Frank. Weekends once consumed by work now held the promise of escape to the fresh, welcoming humidity of the riverbank. The gentle rocking of the boat on the bayou waves, the hours spent talking while waiting for the fish to bite, the spray against his face—these were the antidotes to the city's distractions and the frantic pace at which Frank lived his life. But as far as he was concerned, the true treasure of Isle-aux-Oies resided not in the fish-filled waters, but in the kitchens of Bessie Bellingrath.

Bessie possessed a skill that rivaled, and indeed surpassed, many a professional chef. With plump shrimp, oysters kissed by the Louisiana brine, and an array of fish that shimmered like jewels from the Gulf, she concocted feasts that made even the most jaded palate beg for more, and as the Boykin-Bellingrath partnership and the fortunes of the fizzy black gold flourished, so too did the Bellingraths' cottage. What began as a simple fishing retreat gradually transformed into a wonderland of vibrance. Bessie's love for flowers inspired their bloom in the fertile bayou soil; around their humble abode, rose bushes began to send shoots and blossom. Hibiscus flowers, the color of fiery sunsets, burst forth, adding a tropical touch to the retreat as with each passing season, new additions joined the spread.

In time, this colorful collection of plenty would lay the foundation for the building that would become known as the Bellingrath Gardens, a lasting tribute to the couple Frank so adored.

***

Earlier in 1915, Boykin and Everett had moved back down to Mobile on business. With its rich history, diverse culture, and thriving trade networks, Mobile County was fueled by timber, cotton, and the promise of a prosperous future. Frank's sights were set on a diverse portfolio: livestock raising, timber and lumber production, the extraction of naval stores—a crucial resource for shipbuilding—and the operation of sawmills. They also expanded on the established commissaries, which were small stores that catered to the needs of their employees.

This growth, however, coincided with a complex land ownership situation. Much of the region had been traditionally inhabited and utilized by the Choctaw Native American tribe. The Choctaw lived a settled lifestyle, which had facilitated the development of their agricultural expertise in cultivating corn and squash, and likely surpassing other southeastern tribes. The Indian Removal Act of 1830, however, had forced them to cede their Mississippi lands for territories east of the Mississippi River. Nonetheless, the Choctaw proved to be resilient and shrewd adapters; they adopted European tools and weapons, embraced Christianity to varying degrees, and even developed a written language using the Latin alphabet.

Frank Boykin, ever pragmatic, recognized the potential of their land in Mobile and entered into sharecropping agreements with the tribe. Sharecropping was a prevalent system at the time, where farmers worked a portion of land in exchange for a share of the crops produced; indeed, Frank had come from a sharecropping background himself. With the Chickasaw holdings already in his hand, Frank saw an opportunity for further growth here, as well. While the Choctaw people cultivated the land, the Boykin-Everett partnership gradually acquired ownership of these shares. This shift often resulted from accrued debts at the commissaries, where essential supplies could be acquired on credit. Additionally, some Choctaw families were unable to pay property taxes on their land, leading to its forfeiture.

But Frank was a businessman, and he did what he did best: he turned dust to gold, and opportunity to profit.

Prohibition & Opportunity

A strange time was now at hand; 1920 onwards, the land of opportunity was transformed into a land of absurdity during the era of Prohibition. Imagine a time when speakeasies, hidden dens of iniquity, flourished in the shadows of towering skyscrapers. Saloons, once boisterous hubs of social life, became dusty relics, their doors chained shut by the iron fist of the 18th Amendment. Alcohol, the demonized elixir, became a coveted prize, smuggled across borders in rumrunners' bellies and hidden compartments of automobiles.

The temperance movement, fueled by a desire for social reform, had finally clamped its iron jaws on the nation's thirst. Drunken brawls, domestic violence, and societal ills were attributed solely to the demon rum; little did they know, Prohibition would unleash a Pandora's box of unintended consequences. As once-respectable brewers and distillers were forced underground, bathtubs became makeshift breweries, spewing out potent concoctions that could turn a mild-mannered accountant into a roaring lion (or a very sick individual). Gangsters seized the opportunity, and bootlegging empires flourished, their speakeasies pulsating with jazz music and the clinking of glasses.

The experiment in social engineering had backfired spectacularly. Crime soared, corruption seeped into law enforcement, and the very fabric of society frayed. The quality of alcohol plummeted, leading to a rise in poisonings and health problems. The intended beneficiaries—women and families supposedly terrorized by drunken husbands—found themselves worse off. The speakeasies, catering to a hidden clientele, became breeding grounds for vice and violence.

Of course, even in this time when social liberty was being stepped upon, Frank Boykin knew a guy who knew a guy, and the jaws of a tyrannical amendment held no fear for the veteran Boykin. Within the confines of Frank's room, a party thrummed with a feverish energy, fueled by oceans of bootleg whiskey and bathtub gin that could peel paint. 'Shinny', as this local rotgut was affectionately (or perhaps desperately) called, was the lifeblood of the gathering. Fifteen dollars a quart, a king's ransom for this vile concoction, yet tonight, it flowed like the nectar of the gods.

The revelry reached a crescendo, voices rising in a cacophony that threatened to shatter the plaster walls. But alas, the well of "Shinny" began to run alarmingly low. With a furrowed brow, Frank reached for the ancient telephone by the bed. Its brass surface gleamed faintly in the dim light, the only witness to countless transactions. Into the receiver, Frank's voice, usually smooth as buttered molasses, adopted a tone of urgency. "Now, you listen t'me good, Joe," he bellowed, "'Nother two quarts, pronto! The good stuff, y'hear?"

Downstairs, in the dimly lit lobby the bellboy, known to all as 'Bellboy Joe', scrambled to obey. With dutiful zeal, Bellboy Joe grabbed two bottles.

Meanwhile, Frank put down the receiver, turned around, and beamed at the party. A motley crew of friends surrounded them, each one a tributary feeding the celebratory stream, and it was indeed a cause worthy of celebration: he had a hardwood tract ready to be sold, and the air thrummed with the exhilaration of an upcoming fortune.

As Frank held a crystal decanter aloft, its amber contents catching the sunlight like a captured sunset, a man across from him raised his glass in response. This was the buyer: one Colonel Vernon E. Knight. This wasn't your typical lumber baron; Knight possessed a quiet power, an energy that crackled beneath his calm exterior. Frank, ever the judge of character, once declared him "one of the ablest businessmen". This was true, for the sale of the land meant not just wealth for Frank, but security for Colonel Knight's vast veneer plant. It was a win-win, which was ultimately the best way of making a tidy profit. The clinking of glasses resumed, a toast not just to the deal, but to the camaraderie of two shrewd, skilled businessmen.

There was a knock at the door. As Frank opened the door with a flourish, he was pleased to find Bellboy Joe panting with his white gloves and gleaming brass buttons, a triumphant grin on his face, and two bottles of liquor in his gloved hands. But before this triumphant delivery could be announced to the rest of the party, the door next to Frank's opened. A bewildered furrow creased the brow of the stranger as he emerged from his room.

"I didn't order this," said the man, confused, before noticing the bottle was for Frank.

"Yessir, but I did," said Frank with a good-natured smile. "Frank Boykin, at y'service. Say, how 'bout you come on in and join the party?"

The man, caught flatfooted for a moment, quickly recovered and shook Frank's hand. "Oh, well. I'd be delighted."

A familiar smile creased across Frank's face. "Right this way. Come on in, Mr...?"

"Coleman," the stranger supplied, pleasantly overwhelmed by the sheer force of the Boykin welcome. "Frank Coleman."

Frank, the very picture of Southern hospitality in a linen suit the color of seafoam, ushered him inside. Inside, laughter bubbled over swigs of liquid joy, punctuated by the clinking of ice in highball glasses.

Coleman, intrigued, stepped hesitantly into the whirlwind. He introduced himself as a representative of the United States Steel Corporation, a title that resonated with power in the smoky, industrial landscape of the early 20th century. His mission in Mobile, it turned out, was far from frivolous; he was here on a quest to forge a steel titan on the shores of the city. A colossal shipyard, a leviathan capable of birthing behemoths of the sea, was what he envisioned.

"I've already inspected several sites," Coleman confided as he settled into a plush armchair. "I like one of them very much, but the price is too high, even for the Steel Corporation."

Frank leaned forward, eyes twinkling. He might not have been here for business, but he had never been one to not mix business and pleasure. He remembered the Chickasaw land acquired from the Burgess deal, and he knew instantly: this was his chance. But this was a game, Frank knew, and the game demanded knowing the right people, making the right friends, and taking the right call. Right now, he knew, the right call was looking him right in the face—and an accomplished hunter, Frank Boykin never missed his mark.

"Well, now, have you seen any Chickasaw properties?" Frank asked, his voice steady and confident.

Coleman's interest was piqued. "No, not that I can recall. Tell me more."

And so, Frank told the Steel Corp man the tale of the Chickasaw property rescued and secured from Colonel Burgess' clutches. Frank always had a knack for storytelling; leaning in, he had begun to paint a picture with his words, describing the property in glowing terms, emphasizing its potential, its value. He saw the spark of interest in Coleman's eyes, saw the calculations happening behind that calm facade. This was it—the man was hooked. It was time to go in.

"I say, you should come with me tomorrow up north," Frank said cheerfully. "We could go down to the property ourselves, an' you can see what's what yourself."

Coleman agreed; that night, the party continued and a good time was had by all. The next morning, Frank met up with his namesake, and the duo prepared to leave.

The sun hung low in the sky as Frank Boykin and Coleman set out for the Chickasaw property, its pale light casting long shadows across the landscape. The murmur of the waking world grew steadily distant, and as they drove north of Mobile, the road wound through the dense Alabama woods. Frank, behind the wheel, kept his eyes on the road, but his mind was on the land they were about to visit. He knew providence had played a part in securing him that land, but now it was up to Frank to make good on the opportunity before him.

The car rumbled along the gravel path. Frank stole a glance at Coleman, who sat in silence, eyes keenly taking in every detail of their surroundings. This was a man who missed little, but Frank knew the land was good—he'd let it do most of the talking.

As they neared the property, the landscape began to change. Covered in the sprawling expanses of old-growth trees, the land was raw and untamed, with a potential that Frank had recognized immediately. They pulled to a stop at the edge of a broad meadow, the car's engine falling silent.

Frank stepped out, with Coleman following suit as his gaze swept over the landscape with a critical eye. They walked side by side, their footsteps crunching softly on the dew-kissed grass. Frank began to speak, his voice low and steady, painting a picture of what could be—describing to Coleman exactly how and why this land was best suited to the interests of the firm he represented. Coleman listened, nodding occasionally, but his eyes never stopped moving. They scanned the horizon and assessed the soil underfoot. Frank knew that Coleman was envisioning the future, considering travel costs and distances.

They reached a rise that overlooked the land. Now, Frank stopped and turned to Coleman, gesturing expansively.

"Right, this is it," Frank said, his voice filled with quiet conviction. Moment of truth. "What d'you say, Frank?"

Frank Coleman was silent for a long moment, his face unreadable. Then, slowly, he nodded. "It's good land," he said finally. "What's more, it's exactly what we're looking for."

Frank felt a surge of satisfaction. He knew the deal was as good as done, but he kept his excitement in check. They walked back to the car, discussing terms and details, the practicalities that would turn this vision into reality.

Finally, they shook hands, sealing the deal.

As they drove back to Mobile, the sun climbed higher, burning off the morning mist and bathing the landscape in a warm, golden light.

Many years later, an acquaintance asked Frank whatever happened to that ol' Chickasaw property he'd worked so hard to get.

"Made a reasonable profit on it," Frank replied casually. He didn't elaborate. There was no need.

The fact was that he had sold it for about *seven hundred and fifty thousand dollars*, a tidy sum that exceeded what he had paid by half a million bucks—and that's in 1920s money. And as always, Frank had also reserved the timber and mineral rights for the land, plus five hundred and sixty-five acres of highly valuable property.

The day the shipyard was dedicated was one of celebration for the entire city. Mobilians turned out in masse, their excitement palpable. From Pittsburgh came swarms of executives from the Steel Corporation, their presence a testament to the significance of the occasion. Amidst the exultations, Mayor George Crawford of Mobile turned to Frank, his expression one of sincere gratitude.

"Frank, this is going' to bring new life to Mobile," he said. "This...this will really start us off!"

Frank simply smiled, acknowledging the mayor's words. He knew what this meant for Mobile and how it would transform the region. He had always believed in the potential of this land, and now, that potential was being realized. Now, there was time for festivities and merrymaking on the back of the Boykin-US Steel deal, and as the night wore on, Frank found himself reflecting on the journey that had brought him here. He had turned dust to gold, opportunity to profit. But he was also proud that he had contributed to the growth and transformation of Mobile, had helped to shape its future.

Around him, the party continued, but Frank's mind was already on the next step, the next opportunity. Yet he was not one to fixate too much on the future either; Frank Boykin knew when to stop and smell the roses. After all, this was a landmark day, not just for Mobile, but for Frank Boykin, the man who had made it all possible.

Outside, the stars shone brightly. The world was changing rapidly, but he knew one thing for certain: there would always be opportunities for those who knew where to look.

***

But the festivities were only just beginning for the Boykins—the celebrations of Frank Boykin's professional life were about to synchronize and overlap with his joy as a married man...and father. For indeed, Ocllo Boykin, who had been with child for months now, had delivered not one but two heirs to the Boykin name—John Gunn and James Robert.

The arrival of the Boykin twins, couldn't have been more perfectly timed. Born during the celebrations of the land deal's official closing, they became forever intertwined with this momentous occasion. This, for Frank, was a day of double celebration—a fantastic and meaningful sale, and the expansion of the Boykin family.

The twins brought a new dimension to their lives. Gone were the days of quiet evenings spent solely with each other. The house echoed with the sounds of gurgling babies, the rhythmic rocking of cradles, and the constant murmur of lullabies. Ocllo, ever the picture of quiet strength, embraced motherhood with the same dedication she brought to everything else. Frank, meanwhile, reveled in his fatherly role, showering the twins with affection and already dreaming of the day they'd join him in his business ventures.

This was a time that marked the beginning of yet another chapter for the Boykin family, as Frank Boykin, businessman, timberman, and tycoon, also adopted the role of Frank Boykin the patriarch—a role that suited him like a glove.

The Timber Tycoon

The rhythmic clack-clack of the AT&N train echoed through the dense Alabama forest as Frank squinted through the window at the sun-dappled leaves. Ninety-two thousand acres of untouched wilderness stretched before him, a dormant giant beneath a cloak of ancient oaks and pines. Owned by a distant English firm, this land was nothing if not pure untapped potential, nothing short of a siren song for the timber baron that Frank was fast becoming.

Here, in his element, Frank Boykin wore the uniform of an eccentric—a dappled brown suit over a shirt with sleeves pulled back over broad forearms. His frame filled the suit without a hint of the comfortable spread to come. A shock of dark hair tumbled under a Stetson, its wide brim framing a strong, smiling face. His hands, strong and calloused, tapped a steady rhythm against the train window as he considered the past, the present, and the future.

His crosstie business was going well, profits stacking like cordwood. Now, a bigger game beckoned; with a gambler's grin, Frank had secured the rights to cut timber on this vast tract, unleashing a flurry of activity. Each passing tree wasn't just scenery; it was opportunity, profit waiting to be harvested, and ambition filled in his gaze as he envisioned the coming transformation—this virgin forest, a green sea stretching towards the horizon, would soon be transformed into stacks of wooden gold. This wasn't just land; it was his future, his legacy waiting to be carved out.

Chopping crews materialized seemingly overnight, a flurry of axes and saws carving into the dense forest, leaving behind barren stretches of land. Conventional wisdom had painted a bleak picture of this land; most folks saw it as a barren wasteland, good for nothing but dust and regret. Frank's vision, however, had always been a different breed. When others saw only a depleted forest, he saw potential—the potential for regrowth, for a future where the land would yield its bounty once more, because, for Frank, the key wasn't in maximizing immediate gain. It was in buying when others were blinded by fear, in holding on when doubt gnawed at their resolve. He believed, with unwavering certainty, that this stretch of land surrounding Mobile and along the Tombigbee River held a hidden value waiting to be unearthed.

And he was willing to stake his future on that belief.

The rhythmic thud of his workmen brought only a certain satisfaction to Frank. This was the sound of progress, and Frank was nothing if not a man of progress; he had been born of progress, and damn it all if he would let it pass him by without making a buck—and progress often had a mind of its own, willing men like Frank to keep up with the tide or be left behind.

And just as Frank had expected, the land came back into play. The Roaring Twenties were Frank's savior, as America began its new-age Renaissance. Cars were rolling off assembly lines faster than ever before. Henry Ford's Model T became a symbol of the times—affordable, efficient, and a gateway to freedom on the open road. Meanwhile, everyday Americans, lured by stories of easy riches, poured their savings and borrowed money to play the Stocks game. Stock prices soared, seemingly defying gravity. Shoe shiners dispensed investment advice, and farmers dreamed of mansions. It was a national lottery, fueled by a potent cocktail of optimism and amnesia. The horrors of the Great War were already a fading memory, and the media fanned the flames of this cultural revolution. Radio waves crackled with the latest jazz hits and flapper fashions. Hollywood flickered to life, churning out stories of carefree lives, extravagant parties, and impossible dreams.

And amidst this madness would arrive the real estate frenzy, sending property values into the stratosphere. The fever spread across the nation, infecting everyone from seasoned investors to ordinary citizens with dreams of owning a piece of paradise. People bought land sight unseen, fueled by promises of future development and ever-increasing prices. Empty lots were subdivided and resold at exorbitant prices, with each transaction driving the bubble further, and the banks, eager to capitalize on the craze, loosened lending standards. Mortgages became easy to obtain, even for those with shaky finances. The logic? Land prices would only go up, making repayment a breeze. It was a classic case of speculation gone mad, with no regard for actual value or future sustainability.

The frenzy reached its peak in 1925. Land prices became astronomical, completely detached from reality, and the best part was that Frank was prepared. The land he had acquired suddenly sported a price tag of millions. It was a surreal turnaround, even more so considering the million dollars worth of timber he'd harvested already.

His gamble had become the cornerstone of his fortune as he sold the land for a tidy fortune, establishing the core principle behind his sprawling timber empire: acquire land, harvest the timber, replant in part, and then sell barren land. Over time, his landholdings grew as thousands of acres accumulated, silently growing and enriching his enterprise. They were self-sustaining giants, paying for themselves and promising even greater yields in the years to come. These fertile acres would later become part of a vast conservation program encompassing over 150,000 acres in Washington County and beyond.

His next acquisition was 90% of Dauphin Island for $50,000, and on this sliver of land thrust into the emerald embrace of the Gulf, Frank envisioned a new frontier of his empire. He wasn't alone. The South was rising from the long slumber of Reconstruction, and now, his Washington Lumber and Turpentine Company roared to life. Sawmills hummed, their ravenous blades tearing into the virgin forests. Soon, ships laden with lumber and fragrant turpentine would depart the island, carrying the wealth of Dauphin Island to distant shores.

But he wasn't content with just harvesting the bounty of nature; Frank Boykin was an eccentric man, and he understood the importance of spectacle—thus, the Alabama Deep Sea Fishing Rodeo was born. The turquoise waters teemed with life—marlin, sailfish, the bounty of the deep - just waiting to be hooked. The inaugural rodeo was a roaring success; boats bobbed on the horizon, a colorful armada battling the elements for bragging rights and a hefty cash prize. Newspapers trumpeted the event, and pictures of grinning fishermen hoisting magnificent catches captured the public imagination. In time, Frank and his partners would sell it to the Mobile Chamber of Commerce for a whopping $1,600,000.

But the rodeo, for all its success, was just one piece of the puzzle. In 1934, with pockets lined with profits from lumber and tourism, he established the Tensaw Land and Timber Company. His ambition? To carve out a personal fiefdom, a vast swathe of virgin forest stretching across three counties. Over 100,000 acres fell under his dominion, an emerald cathedral echoing with the cries of unseen birds and the rustle of unseen creatures.

And so, by 1934, Frank Boykin had transformed himself from a corporate climber to a tycoon—he was the richest man in Mobile, standing atop the magic plateau of a seven-figure fortune. John Everett was gone, but Frank, driven by an indomitable spirit, had built another empire.

Yet, beneath the success, a restlessness simmered within Frank Boykin. He had conquered the land and tamed the sea, but a nagging question remained: what next? In time, a single-minded ambition burned brightly within him. Frank and his partner, H.S. Hoover, now purchased 1,500,000 acres of land along the Florida coast for $1.5 million dollars north of Tampa. Lots and houses were sold to hundreds of northerners, brought down by train, and accommodated in the hotels. But the market was tumultuous, and with dubious confidence in it, Frank made a call—he convinced his partner to auction out all the lots in Chicago.

In a single auction, they sold out a million dollars worth of lots—and a few months later, Frank's hunch proved true. The market crashed, and the lots were now worthless.

Part III

The Wartime Congressman

(1935 - 1943)

Man in Office

Frank Boykin, the shrewd businessman who carved an empire from the fertile lands of Alabama, had never envisioned himself wading into the murky waters of politics; indeed, he had not been much interested in politics for much of his career, abstaining from voting for nearly a decade. His world, after all, revolved around land deals, timber contracts, and the relentless pursuit of expansion.

Yet, by 1935, a confluence of factors propelled him onto the national stage, transforming him from a land baron to Congressman Boykin.

The seeds of Frank's political foray were, in part, rooted in his childhood; he had grown up in the south, and he understood the political realities, the people, and the world of Alabama better than anyone. Always a people person, perhaps politics had always been a part of Frank Boykin's destiny.

Then, there was his devotion to business. A staunch advocate of free markets and minimal regulations, he saw unions and worker protections as impediments to economic progress. He was a man who believed in the rugged individualism that had fueled his own success, and he felt a duty to protect this system for future generations. The rise of organized labor movements in the early 20th century, particularly in the North, further cemented his stance against such radical ideas.

However, Frank's foray into politics wasn't solely driven by ideology. Circumstances played a significant role. The Great Depression had ravaged the nation, leaving a trail of economic despair across Alabama. The New Deal policies implemented by President Franklin D. Roosevelt, despite their good intentions, were met with mixed reactions in the South. Many, including Frank, viewed them as an unwelcome intrusion into local affairs. He felt the federal government wasn't doing enough to alleviate the suffering, particularly among the agricultural and business communities.

Then came the unexpected opportunity. In 1935, Congressman John McDuffie, representing Alabama's 1st District which encompassed Mobile, received a federal judgeship appointment. This triggered a special election to fill the vacant seat. Frank, despite not having voted in any election since the 1920s, saw this as a chance to champion his beliefs and influence policy decisions directly, and voters in Choctaw, Marengo, Clarke, Wilcox, Monroe, Washington, and Mobile counties, all included in the district at the time, had chosen Boykin to represent them in the national legislature.

Undeterred, Frank launched a vigorous campaign. He focused on his business acumen, portraying himself as a self-made man who understood the struggles of ordinary people. He promised to fight for policies that would revitalize the local economy, create jobs, and protect the interests of Alabama's citizens. He generously supported local charities, his name appearing prominently on church donation plaques and scholarship programs. Over the years, he had befriended many influential figures, and now he leveraged his business acumen to secure their backing.

Adding a touch of drama to the campaign was the revelation that Frank hadn't paid poll taxes for over a decade. This basic requirement for voting, aimed at preventing voter fraud, suddenly became a hurdle for the aspiring Congressman. In a move that further solidified his image as a man of action, Frank did the unthinkable—he paid fourteen years' worth of back poll taxes in one go.

This audacious act was seen by many as a sign of his commitment and a willingness to play by the rules—even if it was on his own terms.

Election day arrived, a tense culmination of months of tireless campaigning. As the votes were counted, the results came in a nail-biting close race. The results were a surprise to many—Frank Boykin, the businessman with no prior political experience, emerged victorious. His win reflected a mood of discontent with the status quo and a yearning for a leader who understood the challenges faced by the people of Alabama, and as the people celebrated and flocked around the man of action, Frank Boykin declared the phrase that would soon become his catchphrase:

"Everythin's made for love, Alabama!" he declared, and this was a sentence he'd stand behind for the rest of his life.

Driven by a potent mix of ideology, frustration with the federal government, and an opportunistic turn of events, Frank Boykin found himself at the center of the political arena, a viper's nest of competing interests and entrenched power structures. Yet his business acumen, strong personality, and ability to connect with voters had laid the foundation for his political rise, and these very skills would serve him well in the coming years. On the other hand, Frank's isolationist stance, his sympathies for the old South, and his anti-labor stance also threatened to clash with the political realities of Washington. It would take all of the charisma he had to maintain congenial relations with the White House while simultaneously appeasing his new voter base.

Luckily for him, Frank Boykin had charisma in spades.

***

A whirlwind of energy descended upon the office the day Frank took to the chair; gone were the staid routines of the previous administration, replaced by a palpable hum of activity. Aides scurried like busy ants, their paths crisscrossing in Frank's office, the epicenter of this political maelstrom. Frank, a man who'd built an empire on sheer force of will, was determined to do the same with his political career.

He very much understood the importance of alliances, and with the grace of a Southern gentleman, he began weaving a web of connections. Friends and potential adversaries alike were swept up in his charm offensive. Soon, whispers of Frank's legendary soirees began to circulate through Washington's power corridors. Lawmakers, dignitaries, and military brass jostled with business titans for a coveted invitation. The laughter and camaraderie Frank built here served as the mortar that bound these alliances, ensuring his constituents' voices wouldn't be lost in the legislative labyrinth.

True to his word, Frank became a champion for the economic rebirth of Alabama. Infrastructure projects bloomed across the state, promising jobs and a brighter future. He fought tooth and nail for the farmers, securing agricultural subsidies that were the lifeblood of rural communities, and federal regulations, viewed as shackles on local businesses, found in him a fierce opponent. His fiery speeches resonated with his campaign promises, echoing anthems of self-reliance, free markets, and a government that kept its mitts off the gears of progress.

Perhaps his most ingenious strategy was the series of hunting expeditions he hosted on his sprawling Alabama estate. These weren't mere trips into the wilderness; they were opportunities to forge bonds with fellow lawmakers and power brokers. The camaraderie forged over the thrill of the hunt often translated into unwavering support within the halls of Congress. It was a masterstroke, a perfect marriage of Frank's prolific love for the outdoors and his political acumen, further solidifying his reputation as a man who could navigate the political terrain with the cunning of a seasoned fox.

As years flowed by, Frank's signature phrase, "Everything's Made for Love," became a mantra, a rallying cry for his political identity. It resonated with the people of Alabama, and it was a phrase he uttered both to roaring crowds in Mobile and through the hallowed halls of the House floor, a constant echo of the man and the legacy he was determined to build as a man in office.

Yet even as a new reign began in the heart of Alabama and Frank Boykin began a new and exciting time in his long, eventful life, far to the east, unseen by the world, storm clouds were growling—and in a few years, all in America would hear the sound over the pacific: the sound of war and marching drums.

Clouds of War

By the 1930s, the first World War should have been a distant myth, a relic of a past done and dusted nearly two decades ago.

Yet across the ocean, the scars of the Great War still crackled with tension by the mid-1930s. By and large, Europe continued to chug along, but its great economies lay in tatters. Meanwhile, the Treaty of Versailles that had concluded the Great Wars, meant to punish Germany, festered like an infected wound—and it was into this volatile mix that two ambitious dictators, Adolf Hitler in Germany and Benito Mussolini in Italy, began to stir the pot.

Hitler, a charismatic but hate-filled leader, rose to power in the 30s on the back of the simmering effects of the first great war on the German psyche. He came with his machismo, his volatile charisma, and a dark glint in his eye as he addressed the youth of his nation, promising to restore Germany's lost glory. He preyed on the humiliation of the Treaty, blaming it on minorities, whipping nationalistic fervor into a frenzy. By 1934, with alarming speed, the fragile flower of democracy had been devoured by the weed of totalitarianism. The Third Reich, a Reich of lies, terror, and virulent nationalism, had taken root. Meanwhile, in Italy, Mussolini, the "Il Duce", had already established a fascist state, a system that crushed dissent and glorified violence. These men, with their bellicose rhetoric and expansionist dreams, were like hungry wolves eyeing a weakened herd.

The first test came in 1936, when Mussolini, drunk on dreams of a new Roman Empire, invaded Ethiopia. The League of Nations, the supposed guarantor of peace after World War I, sputtered ineffectively. This impotence was a glaring sign—the old order was crumbling. Hitler, emboldened, remilitarized the Rhineland, a region Germany had been forbidden to station troops in. Yet the Western powers, Britain and France, fearful of another war, chose not to act; with their economies slowly returning to normal, and with the fear of another long, bloody conflict, they played the appeasement game—not knowing that to appease a tyrant is to embolden him. And so, all their meekness showed Hitler that aggression wouldn't be met with force.

Then, in Spain, a bloody civil war erupted. Fascist forces under General Franco, backed by Italy and Germany, battled the democratically elected Republican government. This conflict became a testing ground for the new war machine Hitler was building; German bombers rained terror on civilian populations, a tactic foreshadowing the horrors to come.

Yet again, the European democracies, unwilling to intervene for fear of a wider war, simply watched and waited.

As the 30s rolled on, Hitler's ambitions only grew bolder. With each bellicose stamp of his foot, armies moved; he began to absorb neighboring Austria and the Sudetenland, a German-speaking region of Czechoslovakia. Yet again, the appeasement policy of the Western powers emboldened him. At the infamous Munich Conference in 1938, Chamberlain, representing a weary Britain, and Hitler, exuding confidence bordering on arrogance, reached a deeply mistaken accord. The agreement allowed Germany to annex the Sudetenland, effectively severing a portion of Czechoslovakia without its consent.

This was deal with a devil, one that should never had been made—for it was a faux peace, one that only proved to Hitler that he was unopposed. Outside the gilded chambers, in the streets of Europe, murmurs of dissent mingled with anxious anticipation. The Czechoslovakian leadership, sidelined and forsaken by their supposed allies, faced a grim reality: the sovereignty they had fought to defend lay shattered by the stroke of a pen in a distant city.

Chamberlain, upon his return to Britain, declared 'peace in our time,' a statement that would ring hollow. The appeasement policy had failed. Hitler, emboldened by his bloodless victories, saw weakness in the democracies. His appetite for conquest grew, and in March of 1939, he shattered the fragile peace by violating the Munich Agreement and occupying the rest of Czechoslovakia.

Finally, the death-knell of appeasement was at hand; Hitler, emboldened by an alliance with Stalin and the West's continued inaction, turned his sights on Poland. The tinderbox of Europe was about to be ignited—and the flames would once again engulf the world.

***

And so, it happened.

The fragile peace, a cobweb spun from treaties and appeasement, ripped with a thunderclap on the crisp dawn of September 1st, 1939. For the rest of the world, news came slowly yet terribly: German panzers, iron beasts painted the color of war, had roared across the Polish border, their treads churning fertile fields into bloody mud. In Warsaw, cobblestones glittered with the malevolent dew of shattered glass, and Stukas shrieked their death cries as bombs rained down, turning elegant townhouses into smoking pyres. Across the Polish frontier, Church bells, once tolling for morning prayers, now clanged a frantic death knell. Farmers, their faces sagging with terror, scrambled to shield their families in flimsy cellars as the earth exploded in great plumes of mud.

Even as the German Luftwaffe initiated bombing raids on Polish cities and military targets, ground forces advanced swiftly with armored divisions and motorized infantry. In the south, German and allied Slovak troops launched a coordinated assault on the mountainous terrain of southern Poland, exploiting weaknesses in Polish defenses and driving deep into the heart of the country. Despite Polish resistance, including courageous efforts such as the Battle of Wizna and the doomed defense of Warsaw, Poland's outdated military equipment and tactics were no match for the technologically advanced and strategically coordinated German forces. The speed and ferocity of the German assault had caught Poland and its allies entirely off guard.

Now, the dogs of war were let loose, and a grim mobilization began. Across the English Channel, determination settled on the faces of politicians gathered in smoky war rooms. By September 3, both France and Britain had declared war on Germany, and telephones quickly became conduits for frantic diplomacy across continents. The fragile web of alliances, painstakingly woven in the aftermath of the Great War, unraveled with a snap as gas masks were once more distributed, a dark reminder of the horrors of the Great War. Long recruitment lines snaked through the streets, each face reflecting a spectrum of emotions—stoic acceptance, simmering anger, and an excitable, uncomprehending terror in children's eyes. In France, the Parisian cafes now stood eerily silent, chairs turned upside down as conscripts, young men with faces still ripe with the innocence of youth, marched through cheering crowds, the echoes of their boots drumming a war beat upon the heart of Europe.

Meanwhile, in Berlin, a jubilant madness reigned. Flags, emblazoned with the swastika, a symbol twisted into a grotesque parody of a holy cross, fluttered from every window. From loudspeakers, a voice, venomous and hypnotic, promised victory, racial purity, and a new world order. The crowd roared its approval, a wave of fanaticism surging through the streets. Yet the war councils of the Third Reich were all too sober, and immediately after Poland's defeat, Germany focused on securing its newly acquired territories and reorganizing its forces for future operations. The campaign in Poland had shown the effectiveness of Blitzkrieg tactics, which combined fast-moving armored units, close air support, and infantry coordination to achieve rapid breakthroughs and encircle enemy forces.

Now, one of the blood-stained Reich's first strategic moves was to reinforce defenses along Germany's western borders, anticipating potential French and British offensives in response to the invasion of Poland. The construction of defensive fortifications, known as the Westwall, was accelerated to fortify the western frontier against any Allied incursions. At the same time, German strategists under the leadership of Generals such as

Gerd von Rundstedt and Erich von Manstein began planning for the next major offensive: the invasion of France and the Low Countries. Known as Case Yellow (Fall Gelb), this campaign aimed to achieve a decisive victory over France and its allies, thereby eliminating the threat of a two-front war that had plagued Germany during World War I. The great Hun had re-arisen and reborn as an iron monster intent on absolute conquest.

Far away, in America, the war still felt like a distant storm, a rumble on the horizon. Yes, a sense of unease hung heavy in the air, for the news of Adolf Hitler's brazen invasion of Poland had indeed spread like wildfire across the nation, carried by the crackling voices of radio announcers and splashed in bold headlines across the pages of newspapers that fluttered in the hands of anxious citizens. But the memory of the Great War was still fresh in the collective consciousness, and amidst the Great Depression's lingering grip, the idea of entangling the nation in another European conflict seemed unthinkable to many.

As they looked at the newsreels, Political leaders, intellectuals, and citizens alike grappled with a fundamental question: Was this America's fight? On the one hand, debates took bud in living rooms, classrooms, and boardrooms across the nation—but in the jazz bars, the saxophone still rang just the same, and people did their best to go about their day, trying to ignore what was brewing on the other side of the world. Meanwhile, in the Senate, Isolationists cleared their throats and repeated the same tired talking points, like a flimsy shield against the coming tempest.

Yet as the sun remained veiled under a dark morning in 1939, the tireless Frank Boykin sat on his breakfast table with a newspaper before him with another update on the German occupation of Poland and the mobilization of Europe. And as Frank Boykin took his coffee and skimmed the paper, he knew:

Something had to be done.

Wisdom in Sorrow

A hard time was at hand for the Boykin family, but as he breathed in the crisp December air of Washington, D.C., Frank could not have imagined such a thing. The wind held a biting chill that night in 1939, and a reception at the White House was in full swing. When Frank and his wife arrived in Washington, the daffodils were in bloom along Pennsylvania Avenue as though it were spring, and the magnolia trees were out with a smile. But flurries of snow over the next day had culminated tonight as the weather continued to turn and worsen.

Inside the White House, however, the mood was anything but frosty. President Roosevelt, a gracious host, presided over a lively gathering, and Frank found himself caught in a conversation with another senator about the war. His own stance on the war was simple: America had a duty to join. Yet, as a member of Congress during a time when the United States was deeply divided over its role in the burgeoning global conflict, Frank found himself navigating a delicate political landscape.

For one thing, even now, a significant portion of the American public and many of Boykin's colleagues in Congress favored isolationism. The traumatic experiences of World War I had left the nation wary of entangling itself in another overseas conflict. Then there was the economy. Depression had left the American economy in a fragile state, and there was considerable debate over whether the country could afford the economic strain of another major war. But Frank Boykin and Roosevelt were both on the same page despite the risks and the naysayers; they strongly believed in supporting the Allies against the Axis powers. Roosevelt's administration was gradually moving toward greater involvement in the war, even if direct intervention was not yet a popular stance.

For now, Boykin was listening intently as his colleagues voiced their concerns, and the room buzzed with passionate arguments for and against American intervention. Suddenly, he felt a tap on his shoulder, and an usher whispered about an urgent call from Mobile. Frank knew then that it was important; excusing himself, he followed the usher to a quiet corner and picked up the receiver.

The voice on the other end belonged to his brother, Judge Matt Boykin.

"Frank…it's…" he began, and Frank listened.

His son, Frank Jr., was dead, killed by accident by his own hand, by an accidental gunshot. It is hard to imagine what went through Frank Boykin's mind at that moment—standing amidst assembled guests and dignitaries, amidst laughs and revelry as a practiced politician with a near-constant smile, the news must have hit him like a physical blow as he hung up slowly. The reception around him was now a million miles away, but he knew he had to get to Ocllo.

He returned flustered, perhaps still struggling with what to tell her. Knowing that the truth would be too much, especially right now, he did the best he could—he lied.

"We've got to be goin' down to Mobile at once," he said. "Frank Jr.'s been...hurt. We need to go."

Even this was enough to worry her to distraction. Cancelling reservations, the duo decided to fly at once—but the snow had other plans. A blizzard raged outside, grounding all flights. Trapped, they could only wait, the hours crawling by like wounded animals. Anxious and beside herself, Ocllo took the time to send a telegram to their son urging him to fight on. Frank looked away; he still did not have the heart to tell her.

The train journey that followed was an agonizing ordeal. Ocllo spent the night in frantic prayers, and to the couple, each mile that passed likely felt like a decade. They found themselves traveling through the dark mountains, skirting through and around the inky pools of Virginia and North Carolina, before transferring a train to New Orleans. Finally arriving in Mobile after a seeming eternity, the exhausted couple was met by a hushed crowd of worried faces—relatives and friends, all grappling with the impending grief.

Still, Ocllo clung to hope, even as they went to the Boykin residence. But upon entering the familiar living room, a single, unyielding form dominated the space - a cold, grey casket. It was only then, finally, that the truth, monstrous and undeniable, slammed into her.

Her son, her pride and joy, was gone.

A mother's cry escaped her lips as her world tilted on its axis. Frank watched as her knees buckled, by a wave of inconsolable grief—but Frank grieved as well. How had this happened?

But then again, the details, for now, were irrelevant. All that remained was the stark, agonizing truth: his son, their pride and joy, was gone.

***

An ocean away in Europe, daily life had undergone a terrible transformation in the weeks after the declaration of the war. As the dry frost swept through London and Paris, the bustling streets that once hummed with commerce and lively chatter now bore a solemn air, and in their private moments, the people dreaded what may come next.

The onset of war had swiftly tightened the economic belt, forcing governments to implement rationing measures to ensure equitable distribution of scarce resources. In Britain, the Ministry of Food took charge of rationing, issuing ration books to every citizen. Staple foods such as sugar, butter, meat, and eggs were strictly rationed, with families receiving carefully calculated portions that dwindled as the war progressed. Queues stretched outside grocery stores as housewives patiently waited their turn, clutching yellow ration books in anticipation of securing a meager supply of essentials.

In France, the situation mirrored Britain's as government authorities instituted similar measures. Paris, renowned for its culinary delights, saw restaurants and cafes adapting to the constraints of rationing, offering simplified menus and smaller portions. The grand boulevards that once beckoned with elegance now bore the traces of frugality, as Parisians adjusted to life under the shadow of war.

In both countries, smog-choked factories hummed day and night, churning out weaponry, ammunition, and equipment essential to the survival of their nations. Women stepped into roles traditionally held by men, taking up jobs in factories and farms, while families anxiously saw off their young men. Families in rural villages adhered to age-old traditions of preserving fruits and vegetables, storing them in cellar larders against the lean months ahead, knowing with grim certainty that no matter what happened, supplies and rations would surely be disrupted.

But in the occupied territories, life was fraught with uncertainty and danger. The horrors of the Holocaust had not yet begun, but everyday tragedies had begun to set in as hollow-cheeked children watched from windows at the passing

Nazi patrols. As winter settled into its melancholic rhythm, the streets of Warsaw, Kraków, and countless villages bore witness to German military boots clattering on the cobblestones. In the November chill, families huddled in dimly lit homes, their windows shuttered against prying eyes and the chill wind that carried whispers of fear and uncertainty. Food became quickly scarce as rationing measures tightened, leaving pantries barren and stomachs hollow. Outside the cities, farms lay abandoned, their fields fallow and homes shuttered, as families fled or faced forced relocation at the whims of the occupiers.

By the time December arrived with a bitter bite, its frost-covered mornings offered no respite from the relentless grip of occupation. The Christmas of '39 was grey and subdued for these poor souls, and brought little joy to a nation besieged by tragedy.

***

Meanwhile, for the Boykins, the days bled into one another as they struggled with their own, private tragedy. Ocllo remained shrouded in a veil of sorrow. Frank, meanwhile, carried the weight of his grief in the secret regions of his heart, throwing himself into his work—after all, life refused to stand still. Distant obligations tugged at Frank, pulling him back into the public sphere.

He had learned to mask his sorrow, to fold it into the fabric of his daily existence, as he navigated the corridors of power in Washington. The world was at war, yet the United States was still clinging to neutrality. The stakes were monumental, and Frank Boykin found himself at the forefront of a campaign to persuade the American government to aid the beleaguered United Kingdom in its struggle against Nazi Germany. Having lost his own son so recently, Frank Boykin understood far better than most what the Old World would suffer if Hitler had his way and lay waste to Europe. The Reich's war-machine, by all accounts, was ruthless;

Frank's office was a flurry of activity, with aides and clerks bustling about, telegrams arriving in rapid succession, and the phone ringing incessantly. The air was thick with the urgency of the times, and yet, amidst the chaos, Frank exuded a calm determination. His resolve was fueled by a profound sense of duty, not just to his country but to the broader principles of freedom and democracy. The tyranny sweeping across Europe was a threat to the entire free world, and Frank knew that America could not afford to remain on the sidelines.

His speeches were imbued with a passionate plea for action. He spoke of the gallant resistance of the British people, of their unwavering spirit in the face of relentless bombing raids. He painted vivid pictures of the London Blitz, the ruins of Coventry, and the bravery of ordinary citizens in a call to the American conscience. Frank argued that the fate of the free world hinged on the survival of Britain, and that America had a moral obligation to support its ally.

Even behind closed doors, Frank lobbied tirelessly, meeting with senators and representatives and leveraging his political acumen to build a coalition of support. He was relentless, methodically addressing concerns about the risks of involvement, the costs, and the potential for American lives to be drawn into the conflict. Frank countered with the dire alternative: a world where the Axis powers reigned supreme, a nightmare scenario that he described with stark clarity. And even though the isolationist argument still seemed to dominate Congress, Frank's opinion continued to be shared by many, particularly with Roosevelt himself, who knew that something had to be done...and soon.

But for all the chaos in his public life, Frank's private was finally beginning to heal. Slowly, tentatively, a semblance of routine began to reassert itself in the house as Frank and Ocllo got used to their new life. Meals were eaten, the house maintained, and there was a semblance of order amidst the chaos of their hearts. As the weeks turned into months, a subtle shift began to occur. The raw, searing pain of their loss began to dull, replaced by a gentler ache, and the memories of their lost child, initially unbearable, now grew sweeter as the pain dulled. Over the coming years, the life of Frank Jr. would remain a cherished memory, a picture on the mantlepiece of their home together—and their hope, their faith was in the belief that one day, they would be reunited with him in a place beyond sorrow.

Eventually, the year 1939 drew to a close, significant to the Boykins not just for personal tragedy, but for the momentous events unfolding across the Atlantic. As Europe grappled with the harsh realities of war, the fire of conviction continued to burn within Frank. He saw in the plight of Britain a reflection of the potential future America faced if the tide of war wasn't turned. The news from Europe was a constant reminder of the urgency; rationed food, darkened streets, and the ever-present threat of Nazi occupation painted a grim picture of a world teetering on the brink. Each report reinforced Frank's belief that America's isolationism was a luxury it could no longer afford.

Now, as the new year dawned, Frank and Ocllo carried the weight of their grief, but also a newfound hope—hope in a better tomorrow, for even as the world seemed to teeter on the brink, they carried the unwavering belief in the future. The road ahead was uncertain, the fight far from over. But Frank Boykin, forever marked by personal tragedy, knew that the fight for freedom, was a fight worth waging—for it was the gains of freedom that made up for the losses one suffered in life.

Wolf Across the Channel

It was on October 9, 1939, that Hitler issued Directive No. 6 for the Conduct of the War, outlining a grand offensive designed to crush the Allied forces and seize vast swathes of territory in Holland, Belgium, and northern France. These regions, Hitler believed. could be used to launch a sustained air and sea campaign against England. Grand Admiral Erich Raeder, head of the Kriegsmarine, was assigned the daunting prospect of an invasion of Britain. Passing down this pressure, he instructed his operations officer, Kapitän Hansjürgen Reinicke, to study the feasibility of troop landings on English soil should the situation demand it.

Reinicke's subsequent study considered the heavy prerequisites for a successful onslaught upon the British Isles: the neutralization or containment of the Royal Navy's formidable presence in the vicinity, the crippling of the tenacious Royal Air Force, the obliteration of all Royal Navy units in the strategic coastal zones, and the prevention of British submarine actions against the beachhead fleet. If it was to succeed, the German war machine would now have to dismantle the defenses of an empire that had withstood centuries of tumult.

In November of 1939, amid the gathering storm, Luftwaffe intelligence chief Joseph 'Beppo' Schmid prophesied a novel strategy, one that emphasized the paralyzing of British trade through a relentless blockade of imports and devastating assaults on seaports. This bold vision culminated in Hitler's Directive No. 9 on November 29, a mandate that demanded an unprecedented coordination of forces to secure the coast and enforce a suffocating stranglehold on UK ports. The directive called for the deployment of sea mines, shipping attacks, and aerial barrages, which would eventually culminate in the aerial theatre of the Battle of Britain.

But as a biting winter swept across the continent in '39, the Wehrmacht unveiled its own grand stratagem: Nordwest. This audacious plan envisioned a large-scale offensive targeting England's eastern coast, a campaign that would unleash the might of airborne troops and seaborne beachheads comprising 100,000 infantry in the heart of East Anglia. Yet, the Kriegsmarine's response to this grand design was marred by trepidation. The naval leadership, still reeling from the grievous losses suffered during the Norwegian campaign of Operation Weserübung, viewed the proposed invasion with a skeptical eye. The reality of protecting a vulnerable beachhead against the might of the indomitable Royal Navy seemed a perilous, but as always, Hitler's whims overpowered the intelligence of his analysts.

Then came 1940, and with it, the beginning of the fall of France. On a fateful May morning, German bombers carved jagged scars across the dawn sky, the thunder of explosions shattering the fragile peace. In the Ardennes, a seemingly impassable forest, German tanks, spearheaded by the ruthless Panzerkampfwagen, performed a balletic maneuver. They sliced easily through the Maginot Line, the colossal network of fortifications France had poured its faith into, and French soldiers, clinging to outdated tactics and static defenses, were left bewildered.

The Blitzkrieg was a masterclass in terror and disorientation. German paratroopers materialized from the sky, and a desperate scramble ensued. French soldiers, eyes hollowed by exhaustion, retreated under a relentless hail of bombs. The roads were clogged with a desperate exodus of civilians fleeing the mechanized inferno as the proud Champs-Élysées became a desolate highway.

As the City of Lights plunged into darkness, the Germans entered the fallen capital on June 14th, their jackboots echoing on the cobblestones.

Meanwhile, in England, Chamberlain's government had crumbled entirely the moment the Germans had invaded France. On the very day of the invasion, a weary and broken Chamberlain resigned, leaving King George VI with the gravest crisis in British history. Now, Britain turned to a man who had spent years warning of the Nazi threat, a man like Roosevelt and Frank Boykin, who had very well understood the threat posed by Hans. The name of this man was Winston Churchill, and he was not a universally popular choice; indeed, many in the establishment viewed him with suspicion, a maverick with a volatile temperament. But in that desperate hour, Britain craved not a conciliator, but a steely leader, a captain who could steer the nation through the impending tempest.

In his first address to Parliament as Prime Minister, Churchill took to the stand and delivered a speech for the ages. Standing before his people, he declared:

"I have nothing to offer but blood, toil, tears, and sweat." Aside from this he promised nothing, except: *"...victory, at all costs, victory in spite of all terror, victory however long and hard the road may be."*

***

Now, as the summer of 1940 descended upon Europe, a shadow crept across the continent, cast by the swift and brutal successes of Hitler's Wehrmacht. France had fallen with a disheartening swiftness, and the British Expeditionary Force had only narrowly escaped annihilation at Dunkirk. In the wake of these stunning victories, Hitler's gaze fixed intently upon the last bastion of resistance in Western Europe: Great Britain. Operation Sealion, the code name for the planned invasion of the United Kingdom, was conceived amid a whirlwind of military ambition, logistical conundrums, and ideological fervor.

The logistical challenges of launching an amphibious invasion across the English Channel were staggering, however. The narrow strip of water, though merely 21 miles at its closest point, presented a formidable barrier. The Channel's unpredictable weather, treacherous tides, and powerful currents made any crossing fraught with peril. Hitler's High Command, well aware of the enormity of the task, scrambled to assemble the necessary fleet. The Kriegsmarine also found itself inadequately prepared for such an endeavor. The bulk of its vessels were designed for Atlantic warfare, not for the delicate and hazardous operation of ferrying troops and equipment across a heavily defended sea passage—yet the Nazi war machine was adamant about taking out the northern threat.

Indeed, as the summer of 1940 hung heavy as the Nazis arrived at the Pas-de-Calais. The tide of war had turned, and with it, the gaze of the German war machine. Across the narrow Strait of Dover, barely a whisper on the wind, lay England, a defiant island daring them to reach across the water. But the wolf was at the door, and its plan was this: to strangle the flow of lifeblood that sustained England, to sever the maritime artery that pumped life into its war effort. They would turn the Pas-de-Calais into a graveyard for British ships, a gauntlet of steel and fire that no vessel could hope to pass.

Organization Todt, the macabre architect of Nazi ambition, descended upon the French coast like a swarm of locusts. July 22nd, 1940, became the day the earth began to tremble. Grim construction echoed across the land, a bleak hymn to war moaning in the shadows as great guns, their bellies pregnant with destruction, were hauled into place.

The first to be prepared was the 28 cm turrets, their hulking forms squatting menacingly along the coast. By early August, they were operational, hungry eyes scanning the horizon. But these were only the beginning. Seven colossal railway guns, leviathans of steel and fury, lumbered into position. Six 28 cm K5s and a solitary 21 cm K12, a veritable giant with a reach stretching 115 km, loomed large. However, the remaining guns, a motley crew of 28 cm and 24 cm cannons, were of frustrating design for the Nazis. Mobile batteries were plagued by sluggishness, their slow turning and agonizingly long reloading times rendering them ill-suited for the dance of naval combat. Yet, they would do their job, and that is all that mattered to Hans.

But the true harbingers of doom were yet to arrive. By mid-September, four colossal naval batteries emerged from the chaos, each a monument to German might. Friedrich August, a three-headed hydra with 30.5 cm guns, led the pack. Prinz Heinrich followed, a deadly duo of 28 cm cannons. Oldenburg, with its two 24 cm weapons, was a more modest predator, but no less dangerous—and then there was Siegfried. Later renamed Batterie Todt, it was a colossus amongst giants. Two 38 cm guns, behemoths capable of spitting fire across 55 kilometers, stood sentinel, their dark muzzles pointed towards the English coast.

To keep these hungry beasts constantly fed with targets, a network of eyes stretched across the Channel. Spotter planes, soaring hawks dissecting the blue canvas of the sky, pinpointed prey. But the Germans weren't content with eyes in the sky; no, fresh radars were also stationed at strategic points, their electronic gaze piercing the veil of distance. From Blanc Nez and Cap d'Alprech, they could see ships as far as 40 kilometers away, even the smallest British patrol craft daring to creep close to the English shore. As if this wasn't enough, two additional radar sites were added: another DeTeGerät at Cap de la Hague and a monstrous FernDeTeGerät long-range radar at Cap d'Antifer near Le Havre.

Standing on the French coast, the wolf dreamt of English soil. The German Army planned a mobile artillery barrage, which was to follow the invasion. Artillerie Kommando 106, a ravenous detachment of the 16th, would land with the second wave, their maws filled with 15 cm and 10 cm guns. Seventy-two of these smaller guns, alongside twenty-four larger ones, would be unleashed upon the English coast within the first week of Operation Sea Lion. The plans continued to be drawn, and the Nazis continued to efficiently plot their dream of cross-channel conquest.

Yet Britain, an island nation with a proud maritime heritage, enjoyed the inherent strategic advantages of its geography. The Royal Navy, still the world's most formidable sea power, controlled the Channel with a tenacity born of centuries of naval dominance. To ensure a successful landing, the Luftwaffe also needed to secure air superiority. This, coupled with logistical constraints, made many even in the Reich question whether the invasion of England would even be worth it.

But for Hitler, the invasion represented more than a mere military conquest; it was an ideological crusade. Nazi Germany's war machine was propelled by a worldview steeped in notions of racial superiority and manifest destiny. The British, despite their shared Teutonic roots, were seen as the last impediment to German hegemony in Europe. Hitler envisioned a new order on the continent, one that required the subjugation or destruction of all who opposed the Reich. In the Führer's eyes, Britain's defiance was both a challenge and a nuisance. The island nation, standing resolute against the tide of fascist domination, symbolized a beacon of resistance that needed to be extinguished to consolidate Nazi power.

As Hitler licked his haunches and prepared to face the British threat to the north, the propaganda machinery of the Third Reich churned out a steady stream of rhetoric designed to bolster German morale and intimidate the British public. The narrative of inevitable victory and the destiny of the Aryan race were woven into the fabric of Operation Sealion, making it not just a military campaign but a testament to Nazi ideology, and English newspapers printed summaries of Hitler's passionate declarations and warnings to England to *make peace or suffer.* These were summarily ignored by Churchill, who turned his brow south, sharpened his steel, and waited.

And now, as the rest of the world watched with bated breath, the stage seemed set for the coming battle—the battle for the fate of England.

The Greek Fire Plan

Early on one August morning in 1940, the Boykins stirred as always to the booming echo of the reveille cannon. The sound, a daily ritual that rattled the windows of their D.C. home, marked the start of another day. Frank Boykin, a man of routine, rose promptly and marched towards the kitchen. There, amidst the comforting hiss of the percolator and the warm aroma of grits simmering on the stove, awaited his *first breakfast*—a potent elixir of strong coffee, its bitterness a stark counterpoint to the creamy sweetness of the grits.

Across the room, his wife, Ocllo, sat bathed in the soft glow of a reading lamp. In her hands, she held a well-worn copy of the Mobile Register, their hometown newspaper delivered all the way from Alabama. As she flipped through the crisp pages, nestled in her armchair, the newspaper became a portal to a world beyond the confines of their Arlington home. Her eyes, keen and intelligent, would flit across the pages, absorbing the local news, the national headlines, and the snippets of society gossip. But this morning, her attention was snagged by a more peculiar enticement—a column nestled amongst the humdrum of everyday news: *A Hundred Years Ago Today.*

Intrigued, Ocllo settled deeper into her chair, glancing briefly at her husband before she began to read aloud a story from another time.

***

Nearly a century ago, the languid heat of the southern summer clung heavy in the air, a thick soup of humidity that seemed to press down on McGrew's Shoals. Here, on the placid face of the Tombigbee, history was soon to be set in motion by one unassuming J.M. Cooper. He, heading a ragtag crew of Albanians, Italians, and even a smattering of local men, was tasked with damming McGrew's Shoals and taming the terrain. But now, Mr. Cooper stood bewildered. His intended well-drilling operation had taken a spectacularly unexpected turn, for, at a depth of 375 feet, the earth had almost swallowed his auger whole. A disquieting silence followed, thick with tension.

Then, a tremor. A low rumble began deep within the earth, growing in intensity until it resembled the distant roar of a summer storm. From the newly formed opening in the ground, a geyser of sorts erupted. But instead of the expected muddy deluge, a clear, shimmering liquid surged forth. It was unlike anything Mr. Cooper, or anyone else gathered around, had ever witnessed. Panic seized the men. Some scrambled for higher ground, eyes wide with a fear he understood too well.

Meanwhile, the fluid flowed with a translucent, almost ethereal quality. As it spilled onto the water's surface, it bubbled and churned, mimicking the frenzied activity of a pot reaching a rolling boil. The sluggish current of the Tombigbee, for once overwhelmed, failed to contain this unexpected bounty. It was a serpent of obsidian, a liquid darkness writhing on the surface, a spectacle both mesmerizing and unsettling as the oil began to spread, a shimmering film creeping steadily outwards.

Uneasy and uncertain, the men set about now in a blur of frantic activity. They erected crude barriers, channeling the viscous, shimmering oil down a tributary towards the swamps further south. They worked like men possessed, driven by a primal fear of the thing; then, news filtered down from the river patrol—a war party from one of the many scattered Native nations had been sighted in the area.

In the cover of the terrain all too familiar to them, the Natives took torch to the pitch-choked water—and in an instant, the most extraordinary event occurred: *the river caught flame.* The film of oil ignited a fiery tissue dancing across the water's surface with a captivating life of its own. The flames, though stopping at a mere six inches in height, were mesmerizing as they bobbed over the skein of the water, offering a spectacle of rare and mesmerizing beauty. The light cast a warm glow on the surrounding scene, painting the coming nightfall with a crimson brilliance.

The inferno raged for three days, a fiery testament to the power the natives had unleashed, and men and women traveled from neighboring towns and homesteads to view the awesome and terrifying spectacle. When the flames finally died down, leaving behind a blackened wasteland where a river once flowed, a chilling silence descended. The devastation was complete; blazing oil had enveloped the vast swamps along the river, cremating hundreds of deer, bear, and small game.

Feathered folk, turkeys, quail, and owls, fleeing the holocaust, were de-feathered or destroyed. Thousands of trees, fine timber, along the river's edge were burned to ashes.

Now, as the men huddled around the ashes, few knew or understood how *ancient* the sight they had seen was, or that it would occur yet again.

For what they had seen, had been a vision as old, perhaps, as war itself.

Fire had always been a weapon. Beginning with naught but flame-tipped staffs in the Stone Age, the Assyrians, as early as the 9th century BC, were employing advanced incendiary arrows and pots. These early devices often contained combustible substances surrounded by caltrops or spikes and were launched via catapults. Such weapons were not unique to the Assyrians; the Greco-Roman world also extensively utilized them. One of the earliest recorded uses of a mechanized incendiary device is mentioned by Thucydides in 424 BC, where during the siege of Delium, a long tube on wheels was used to project flames forward using a large bellows. It was from these ancient, enterprising, and warlike people that a name came for this flammable elixir:

Greek fire.

The original Byzantine sources called the substance a variety of names, such as *sea fire* (Medieval Greek: πῦρ θαλάσσιον pŷr thalássion), *Roman fire* (πῦρ ῥωμαϊκόν pŷr rhōmaïkón), *war fire* (πολεμικὸν πῦρ polemikòn pŷr), *liquid fire* (ὑγρὸν πῦρ hygròn pŷr), *sticky fire* (πῦρ κολλητικόν pŷr kollētikón), or *manufactured fire* (πῦρ σκευαστόν pŷr skeuastón)

Many years later, the strategic deployment of Greek fire came at a pivotal moment for the Byzantine Empire. Weakened by prolonged conflicts with the Sassanid Empire, the Byzantines faced the rapid advance of Muslim conquests. By the 670s, the Arabs had captured Syria, Palestine, and Egypt, and were threatening Constantinople. Greek fire proved decisive in repelling the Arab sieges of the city in the late 7th and early 8th centuries. Its use extended to later naval battles and internal conflicts, notably the revolts in 727 and the rebellion led by Thomas the Slav in 821-823, where the Byzantine central fleet employed Greek fire to devastating effect.

The legacy of Greek fire persisted through the centuries, with mentions of its use continuing into the 12th century. Anna Komnene vividly described its deployment against the Pisans in 1099, though by the time of the Fourth Crusade in 1203, the actual use of Greek fire seems to have diminished. One notable 13th-century account describes the Saracens using a similar substance against Crusaders during the Seventh Crusade, illustrating its enduring fearsome reputation.

The importance of the tactic remained popular even in the Elizabethan age. On May 28, 1588, the Spanish Armada set sail under the admiralty of the Duke of Median Sidonia, who was thirty-eight years old. He was the richest landowner in Spain and had little sea experience. The Santa Martin was the flagship. The Armada would sail through the English Channel and anchor off Dunkirk. There, they would rendezvous with the Spanish army in the Netherlands, led by Alexandro Farnese of Parma, the most successful general ever sent to the Netherlands by the king of Spain. Then, the reinforced armada would turn around and sail due west straight into the estuary of the river Thames. There was a report of 129 ships.

Queen Elizabeth was devastated in that England only had 38 ships. She saw no way to fend off the invasion—thus, the English decided to attack at sea rather than wait for an invasion on land. They set sail to meet the Armada which had headed to Portsmouth.

Sir Francis Drake, sailing on the Revenge, and Lord Howard on the Ark, led the way into battle. They pushed the Armada back toward France, where they planned to resupply and pick up the small landing barges with 130 troops on each for the invasion. The English decided to send six ships set on fire under full sail toward the Armada with loaded cannons. The Spanish sent small boats out to tie up to them and pull them away, but the fire eventually set off the cannons, and the small boats and their crews were blown away. The fireships continued on, and the Spanish fleet fled in horror in every direction. The battle was lost, and the invasion was *foiled by fire*.

Thus, the strategic importance of incendiary weapons in ancient warfare was not to be underestimated. Its development and deployment not only shaped military tactics but also highlighted the great Byzantine Empire's reliance on technological innovation to defend against formidable foes from across its vaulted borders.

Century after century, generals would set the sea aflame against the enemy of their time, and each time as the flames would dance upon the water's surface, casting flickering shadows on the faces of the onlookers, one thing would again and again become certain: the earth held its secrets.

But what is the secret of Greek Fire? This was a closely guarded secret of war for every country that knew the recipe. Greek Fire is the combination of crude oil and Naptha, which is derived historically from the fractional distillation of coal tar and peat, both readily available in ancient times. This combination is highly flammable and will ignite when it comes in contact with water.

Indeed, if Germany had been successful and had defeated the British Isles, Germany, by default, would have complete domination and complete control of Canada, Australia, New Zealand, South Africa, India, and many Asian cities. Central and South America would also have been defeated easily, and Hitler would be at the United States borders both north and south, with Japan coming at us from the west. The domination of the whole world was at stake, and no one *anywhere* had a plan of how to defeat the nazi invasion of Great Britain.

If not for the quick thinking of a concerned United States congressman, Frank Boykin, Great Britain would have been conquered Great Britain and the United States would have no place in Europe to stage war against Hitler.

The domination of the whole world was at stake, and what was needed in the hour was the ingenuity of a true general.

***

And indeed, it was a general in a politician's coat that sat listening on the sofa as Ocllo Boykin read the account out loud. In the dimly lit study, the early morning light filtering through the curtains, Frank Boykin listened to the story in rapt attention, his brow furrowed the way it was when a stroke of brilliance was on the way. After a long and prosperous marriage, however, Ocllo Boykin, too, had the same mind as her husband, and as she concluded the tale, the Boykin couple glanced up at each other. Between them, the air was thick with the scent of freshly brewed coffee, and the beginnings of a daring and brilliant idea.

"Frank," said Ocllo, "I do think this thing has given me an *idea*."

"I'll bet you anythin', dear, that it is the very same as mine," replied Frank.

Why, they asked each other, couldn't the British set the English Channel afire—just as the

Tombigbee River had been set afire years ago—and destroy the German invasion fleet and barges loaded with troops, tanks, and guns? It was a bold and audacious plan, one that seemed almost too fantastic to be real. The possibility and uncertainty of their plan weighed upon them in the morning pregnant with such possibilities.

Frank leaned back in his chair, the wooden frame creaking under his weight. "Well, worry you not, for I'm goin' to do something about it *right now*. It may well be five in the mornin', but I need to make me a call," he said, his voice resolute. He reached for the rotary phone on the desk, the polished brass glinting faintly in the dawn light. He dialed the number of his close friend, Joe Danziger, who lived in Fort Worth, Texas, and was one of four Danziger brothers, all oil men who had lived with oil all their lives. If anyone could provide insight into the feasibility of their idea, it was Joe. Frank listened to the rhythmic clicks of the rotary dial and the steady buzz of the connection, his mind racing with anticipation.

Finally, the call connected. "Joe, that you? It's Frank Boykin, you hear? Boykin, yes. Much apologies fo' the early hour, but this is urgent."

Joe's voice crackled over the line. "Frank, what's goin' on?"

Frank wasted no time, explaining their idea in detail. He described the image they had envisioned: the English Channel, a formidable barrier, turned into a sea of fire, impassable and deadly for any invading force. The flames would consume the German fleet, thwarting their plans and saving England from the imminent threat. Joe listened carefully, his silence indicating deep thought. Frank could almost hear the gears turning in his friend's mind as he weighed the logistics and practicality of such an endeavor.

"So?" Frank said finally. "What d'you say, Joe?"

After a few moments, Joe's voice came through. As Ocllo Boykin listened from across the room, Frank and Joe continued to discuss heatedly, then exchanged a few more details before ending the call. Frank turned to Ocllo, who had been listening intently, her eyes reflecting the dawning light of hope.

"Well?" she asked.

"He says yes," Frank said, smiling grimly.

The general now had his plan; now, all that was needed was to head down to the White House and detail it to the men in those vaulted halls.

***

Two hours later, Frank had received a five-hundred-word telegram from Joe explaining exactly what to do. The plan, in short, would require dumping enormous quantities of oil on the Channel waters and setting it afire with incendiary bullets and flares.

Armed with the telegram, Frank hailed a taxi at the Capitol, urgency tightening his grip on the folded message. As the car sped through the streets of Washington D.C., past monuments and historic buildings bathed in morning light, he scarcely imagined the weight of the world drama accompanying him. Arriving at the White House, Frank presented his credentials to the stern-faced guard at the gate. He was swiftly escorted through a labyrinth of corridors, each turn bringing him closer to the heart of American power. Presidential secretary Marvin McIntyre greeted him with a curt nod and, upon hearing the nature of Frank's mission, led him directly to the Oval Office.

President Franklin D. Roosevelt, seated behind his iconic desk, looked up with curiosity as Frank entered. The room was filled with the faint aroma of tobacco and the distant murmur of advisors in the adjacent rooms. Frank handed over the telegram with a steady hand. Roosevelt's eyes scanned the document, his expression growing more intense with each line he read. His eyes flicked up, his thoughts clearly churning; Frank knew the President was a man after his own heart, and understood his idea's potential almost instinctively.

"Frank," the President finally said, his voice thoughtful and grave, "I want you to see Lord Lothian, the British Ambassador, at once and have him read this telegram. Tell him exactly what you've just told me. This information is too valuable to keep away from the British. Say nothing to anyone about this."

With a firm nod, Frank left the White House, the gravity of the mission settling over him like a cloak. He hailed another taxi, the driver sensing the urgency in his tone as he directed him to the British Embassy. The streets blurred past, a cacophony of city life that seemed strangely distant from the critical task at hand. At the ostentatious and well-maintained British Embassy, Frank was met with immediate recognition. The White House had alerted them of his arrival ahead of time, and he was ushered into a stately room adorned with portraits of British royalty and dignitaries. Lord Lothian, the British Ambassador, stood by the window, his demeanor calm but expectant as they shook hands firmly.

"What can I do for you, Mr. Boykin?"

"This visit's more about what *I* can do for *you*," Frank said as he handed him the telegram. "You'll be wantin' to read this."

The ambassador's eyes widened slightly as he read Joe's telegram, his features tightening with focus. Without a word, he moved to the telephone and placed an urgent call to London. The transatlantic connection crackled with static as he conveyed the critical plan, his voice steady but charged with the importance of the message.

Frank stood by quietly, glancing out of the window at the pale spires of Washington DC. This was a moment that could alter the course of history—an act of Boykin's tenaciousness that was destined to echo through both the halls of power and the battlefield-to-be on the other side of the Atlantic.

World on Fire

The summer of 1940 had crackled with tension across the English Channel; indeed, the second week of July had seemed an eternity of worry and defiance for the beleaguered British Isles. The shadow of Nazi Germany loomed large, and the verdant fields of Sussex – specifically the towns of Eastbourne, Bexhill, and Hastings – became the potential frontline of a fight for national survival.

Major General ECA Teddy Schreiber would be in command of the 134th and 136th Brigades of the 45th Division. These were the men entrusted with the defense of a coastline ill-prepared for the horrors that might befall it; indeed, a June inspection by Brigadier General Georg W. Sutton had painted a grim picture—*'weak'* was his damning verdict. The rolling hills behind the beaches, the natural ramparts known as the Downs, were left to the ragtag band of the Home Guard.

Their defenses, a desperate bricolage of tree trunks, old motor cars, farm carts, and barbed wire trestles, spoke volumes of the nation's hurried preparations. Yet, their orders were clear, stoic, and inarguable: *To hold position to the last man and to the last cartridge.*

On Wednesday the 17th, Lieutenant General Sir Alan Brooke, the man tasked with safeguarding southern England, met with the indomitable Winston Churchill. Doubts gnawed at Brooke. General Edmund "Tiny" Ironside, the overall commander of UK home defense, had devised a strategy, but Brooke wasn't convinced. Churchill, ever the optimist, had envisioned a German landing on the eastern shores, north of a bay called The Wash. But on that fateful Wednesday, a seed of doubt began to sprout in his mind – what if Hitler aimed for the South instead?

Unbeknownst to them, across the English Channel, a decision had been made. The day before, Hitler, the architect of this impending storm, had chosen his target: in the Berlin war office, a line had been drawn from the Reichstag to the Isle of Wight. Meanwhile, on the northern shores of the conquered France, the German navy had amassed 1,900 barges, 168 merchant ships, 386 fishing ships, and 1600 motorboats—a massive armada fit for a historic undertaking.

Hitler amassed a million or more Nazi troops all along the French and Belgium coasts, ready to pounce once the beachhead and harbor were acquired by the 60,000 Nazi troops crossing the English Channel by barges.

However, their rudimentary landing ramps meant they were beholden to the moon and tides. S-Day, the designated invasion date, had to fall within a narrow window: between August 20th and 26th or September 16th and 26th. Any later, and the specter of autumn storms loomed, jeopardizing the entire operation. The planned invasion of Russia in 1941 added another layer of urgency; a delay meant a postponement until spring, and it was a decision Hitler would not forgive.

The man whose neck was placed on the line was Erich von Manstein, a rising star in the German military who had been the architect of the lightning assault through the Ardennes. This Nazi of the hour was chosen to spearhead the attack on the Sussex coast, supported by Manstein's 38th Army Corps. In a show of pomp typical of the Nazi machine, the 18th landing zones, Bexhill and Eastbourne, were chosen to echo the disembarkation points for Julius Caesar in 55 BC and William of Normandy in 1066. Meanwhile, the 34th Division, the first wave, would face a daunting gauntlet. Under the cloak of smoke, they would disembark from rubber boats and small launches, charging towards Pevensey Sluice. There, a formidable British defense awaited: gun emplacements, tank traps, barbed wire, and a minefield.

The Germans approached this challenge with an infantry contingent of roughly 60,000 men. This formidable force would be backed by an impressive arsenal of cars, lorries, motorbikes, tanks, anti-tank guns, howitzers, and mortars. Surprisingly, the division also carried a cavalry contingent of 4,000 horses and 2,000 bicycles, a relic of pre-modern warfare. Meanwhile, the 26th Division would land alongside the 34th, aiming for a pincer movement. Adding a layer of deception, Brandenburg Regiment commandos, disguised in captured British uniforms and fluent in English, would infiltrate enemy lines, sowing chaos, and confusion. Furthermore, forty tanks were earmarked to support the 34th's three-pronged assault. One prong would veer inland, aiming to sever British defenses at Lunsford's Cross. Another would turn south, attempting a surprise attack on Bexhill from the rear. These forces would eventually link up with the 1st Mountain Division, slated to land further east at Combe Haven.

Leading the charge at Bexhill would be none other than Manstein himself, whose tactical brilliance had been instrumental in the fall of France. His peers and even British military historians like Basil Liddell Hart considered him the most capable strategist in the German army. If the Nazis were to land, the British defenders would find themselves faced with Manstein's tactical overland genius—but first, the fleet had to get across the fickle Channel itself.

On the 19th of July, the Reichstag was lit in red and gold as Hitler delivered his now-infamous "Appeal to Reason" speech, a veiled threat to the Isles masquerading as a peace offering. It was a performance met with disdain in Britain, and only an hour later, a BBC statement from London declared that the offer was rejected.

The die was cast.

Meanwhile, the veil of secrecy began to lift. British Ultra codebreakers, the unsung heroes of the war, had cracked the German code, and Operation Sea Lion was no longer a mystery. Though Churchill's hunch had proven correct, he could not afford to gloat; even now, the exact location of the landing remained frustratingly elusive. Yet in the face of this revelation, a decisive change in command took place; Brooke was now given the reins, and the Home Guard's pathetic barricades were bolstered with concrete and sandbags, even as the men were given better weapons. It was a meager improvement, but an improvement nonetheless.

A series of air raids and scuffles had intensified over England, and the British public watched the skies for bombers with scared, tired eyes. Those in the south, huddled on the grey coasts of Cornwall, watched south with the same trepidation felt by their Saxon ancestors centuries ago as they awaited William of Normandy, planning his conquest of the Isles. Yet Churchill's voice continued to boom across the British Empire on the radios, as he famously promised: *"We shall fight on the beaches, we shall fight at the landing grounds, we shall fight in the fields and in the streets, we shall fight in the hills; we shall never surrender."*

As the months passed and the threat of war in Britain itself loomed closer, Churchill grew grimmer and more taciturn still in his speeches. The forerunners of the Blitz—localized air raids, scouting plans, violation of airspace—had already begun, and fear was beginning to take root in the English heart. Now as the Nazi threat continued to grow darker, Churchill spoke up with a message directed entirely at the warmonger—and what a message it was.

It was the ninth of September, 1940, as a London bruised purple by dusk settled into another uneasy night. The acrid tang of cordite, a legacy of the day's air raid, mingled with the damp chill that crept in from the Thames. In living rooms across the city, huddled figures gathered around crackling wirelesses, the faint orange glow of the dials their only illumination. Then, the unmistakable rumble of a deep, clipped voice sliced through the static, and it was the voice of England, the voice of Churchill.

"What he has done," Churchill said in a voice of dignified rage, *"is to **kindle a fire** in British hearts, here and all over the world, which will **glow** long after all traces of the **conflagrations** he has caused in London have been removed. He has **lighted a fire** which will **burn** with a steady and **consuming flame** until the last vestiges of Nazi tyranny have been **burnt** out of Europe."*

The metaphor of the flame was relentless, and to an observer in the know, quite on the nose— and to the unwary Nazis, was a hidden threat that spoke of the British intention to abide by the design concocted by the unlikeliest of war planners, who sat in Washington D.C nursing a cup of coffee as he read the papers, tracing the course of the conflict as it converged upon its climax on the English front.

Things seemed to be reaching a head, and Frank Boykin hoped that the plan to burn the channel had been enough—for if it wasn't, it was the *world* that might burn instead.

***

On the afternoon of September 7, the ominous drone of engines filled the sky over the English Channel. The Luftwaffe's formidable fleet of bombers and fighters, dark and menacing, roared toward their target: *London*. The sun dipped low, casting a golden hue across the waters before it lowered down into the sea, right off the cliffs of Dover. As twilight descended, the first wave of German aircraft breached the serene British airspace as the whine of Stuka dive bombers and the steady hum of Heinkel and Dornier bombers grew louder, their shadows flickering against the backdrop of a crimson sky. London's residents braced themselves as the sirens blared, not yet realizing that this was the beginning of a relentless assault that would last for fifty-six grueling nights.

The Blitz had begun.

For nearly two months, the heavens above London would be transformed into a nightmarish theater of war. Each evening, wave upon wave of Hitler's aerial armada descended upon the city, their bellies heavy with payloads of high-explosive bombs and incendiaries. The Luftwaffe, like a flock of vultures, would swoop in with a singular purpose: to spew death and destruction upon the city of kings.

As the first bombs fell, the impact was immediate and devastating. Buildings that had stood for centuries crumbled to rubble, their once-proud facades now heaps of twisted metal and broken stone. Flames licked the sky, casting an eerie glow over the city and shrouding it in a haze of smoke and ash. The air was thick with the acrid smell of burning, mingling with the cries of the injured and the desperate wail of sirens. The people of London, however, were not easily cowed. In the face of unimaginable terror, they displayed that English hardiness as night after night, they sought refuge in the Underground stations, transforming the labyrinthine tunnels into makeshift communities. Families huddled together on narrow benches, sharing whispered conversations and scant rations, finding solace in their shared plight.

Historians, for years, would remain flummoxed by a simple question, however: why did Hitler not invade England now? It is believed that Operation Sea Lion was indefinitely deferred, yet there would be no point in such a postponement. The fact of the matter is that there was an attempt: The Nazi war machine attempted a single landing on the southern coast, and this is what happened to it.

***

On September 16, 1940, the Nazi fleet set off on the planned route. Hard-eyed soldiers, nazis, and conscripts lined the decks of the boats as they looked across the channel, expecting that for these short hours, they would be safe—that hell would only begin once they landed on the beaches, hopefully, to ram through the ramshackle British lines...

But this did not happen.

As dusk approached, the quietude of the waters was shattered by the distant hum of engines, pricking the ears of the fleet as the Nazis braced for missiles, unaware of the hell that awaited them. Above them, the RAF bombers, sleek and formidable, soared in formation, their mission clear and unforgiving. From their high-altitude vantage point, the pilots could see the German invasion armada below. The ships, packed with soldiers eager to fulfill their orders, cut through the waters like a dark, menacing fleet. Little did they know, their fate was sealed by the very air they breathed; loaded with oil and incendiary bombs as per the recommendation of Joe Danziger and Frank Boykin, the bombers were about to turn the tranquil Channel into a hellscape.

The first wave of bombs fell with practiced precision; canisters of oil splashed onto the surface of the water, spreading rapidly to form an unbroken slick of black. The German soldiers, eyes wide with confusion, watched as the oil spread around their vessels, a dark omen in the twilight. Cries in German filled the air as commanders cried out to each other, shouting over each other as chaos mounted. Ineffectual surface-to-air fire commenced, but the flak was imprecise and a poor deterrent. As the Nazis watched, horrified, the bombers circled back, this time unleashing flares and incendiary bullets. The first flare ignited the oil with a searing brightness that momentarily turned night into day. Flames roared to life, hungrily consuming the oil and leaping onto the ships with terrifying speed.

Panic swept through the German ranks, and as screams of agony pierced the darkness, the wide-eyed eyes of the would-be-invaders reflected no glory, no victory, nothing but flames. Most of the 60,000 Nazis troops and all of their equipment went to the bottom of the channel that night.

Hitler did call off the Operation Sealion invasion only it was on the next day September 17th after his invasion was defeated. His reported 60,000 troops and 1,900 barges at the bottom of the English Channel. This was Hitler's first defeat, he was humiliated and kept the defeat a secret from the German population.

***

The next day, a nurse named Renee Meurisse stood at the threshold of chaos, her white nurse's outfit darkened and grimy in her smoky, blood-streaked surroundings. As a Belgian Red Cross nurse, she was well accustomed to the horrors of war, but nothing had prepared her for what she encountered that day.

As the sun had dipped below the horizon, painting the sky in hues of orange and red, Renee had received an urgent summons to the Brussels station. Expecting a train filled with Belgian refugees, she hurriedly gathered her medical supplies and rushed to the platform. To her astonishment, a German Red Cross train, not a Belgian one, pulled into the station with a piercing screech of metal. Forty coaches, each bearing the swastika, stretched out before her. A weary Nazi officer, his uniform disheveled and eyes blood-shot and maddened, approached Renee. "Help us," he said in, his voice harsh and desperate. "My men are dying!"

Renee's heart skipped a beat, but she could hardly refuse the Germans. She immediately sent out a call for more nurses and ambulances. The Brussels station, quickly turned from a refugee care center to an active battlefield hospital, and as they began unloading the wounded, the air filled with the gut-wrenching sounds of moans and screams. The cries of agony reverberated through the station, mixing with the harsh clang of stretchers being laid out.

Among the first to be carried off the train was a young member of the Wehrmacht, his body horribly burned so that his head and shoulders were a patchwork of charred flesh. Renee, alongside a doctor, carefully placed him in a corner. Determined to understand what had transpired, they decided to coax the story out of him, piece by piece. She knelt beside the soldier, her voice gentle yet insistent, but his answers came in labored breaths, each word a struggle against the pain. "What about your wounds? How did you get like this?" she pressed on.

"We were told...we were going to invade Britain," the young man whispered, his eyes reflecting a distant horror. "They said...nothing could stop us. It was just a matter of...of getting into the boats and crossing the Channel. But...it was *horrible*."

"What did you see?" asked Renee, her throat dry as she looked at the man's face.

"*I saw a world on fire*," he replied in an empty voice, looking off into nothing. "The whole Channel was in flames. The British...bombed us. *Hell couldn't be worse.*"

With those final, tortured words, his life slipped away. Throughout the night, Renee and her fellow nurses worked tirelessly, tending to over five hundred German soldiers. Many of the soldiers they cared for did not survive; their lives extinguished far from the front lines they had been promised to conquer, having died in service to a wretched man who sat far away in Berlin, raging at his men for having failed his plan to invade the Isles.

In a moment of stillness, the Belgian nurse reflected on the futility of the enemy's false dreams—the dreams of conquest, the promises of racial hegemony, all shattered in the face of human suffering. Hitler's men had paid the price, but even as she regretted the loss of life, she was glad, at least, that yet another country would not fall to the Nazis the way hers had.

Churchill requested Roosevelt to keep the details of the method used to defeat Hitler a secret.

***

The men at McGrew's Shoals on the Tombigbee over a century ago could never have imagined that they had played a part in foiling Hitler's plans. By a taking a page from their book, the Boykins had changed the course of history; coming from little, Frank Boykin had ended up becoming the man who burned down Hitler's plan for world conquest.

In a letter to the Mobile Register in 1944, Frank's co-partner, Joe Danziger later said this of the thwarted Nazi invasion:

> It is to Frank and his alertness that all credit is due—in grasping the importance of ideas suggested to him and acting upon them immediately. The State of Alabama can well be proud of your great Congressman and our only regret is that he does not hail from Texas."

But there was another message received by Frank Boykin in his home long after the English Channel was doused and the failed invasion was comfortably on its way to becoming history. As the ever eccentric Frank took a breath between his many calls, laughing with friends and congressmen, promising improvements to his constituents, and planning hunting excursions with men of note, he realized he had an unread note on his desk, most likely forgotten in the tumultuous efforts of the day that constantly competed for his attentions. Clearing his throat and smoothing his mane of greying hair back, Frank Boykin flipped the note open.

Upon it were only the words:

DEAR FRANK

YOU ALWAYS WERE AN EARLY BIRD

FDR.

Part IV

Epilogue

(1944 - 1945)

In 1944, Frank again found himself in the company of President Roosevelt. After shaking his hand, the President said to him, "Frank, I think you ought to know that *your idea* was used. It served its purpose. Amply." Frank only nodded in response, and that was enough.

After the war, Frank Boykin continued his trajectory of influence in politics, though not without setbacks. When, in 1946, the sudden death of Senator John Hollis Bankhead II opened a vacancy in the Senate, Frank saw this as an opportunity to elevate his influence. However, despite his vigorous campaign and considerable local support, Boykin's senatorial aspirations were thwarted; yet in typical Boykin fashion, even though the defeat was a significant blow, Frank took it on the chin and moved on. The loss had done little to diminish his fervor for public service, and he knew he would have another chance.

And indeed, by 1951, the political tides had turned in Boykin's favor. With the retirement of Sam Hobbs, Boykin ascended to the position of the longest-serving member of Alabama's delegation in the House of Representatives. His tenure was marked by a deep commitment to his constituents and an ability to navigate the strange and esoteric corridors of legislative politics. Boykin's influence in Congress could not be overstated during this time, and his efforts often centered on economic development and resource management, reflecting his background and interests.

By the 1950s, the South was roiling with change and resistance in equal measure. The U.S. Supreme Court's landmark decision in Brown v. Board of Education had declared the doctrine of "separate but equal" unconstitutional, setting off a firestorm of opposition throughout the Deep South. Yet even though he was a signatory of the Southern Manifesto, Frank's signature on the document was little more than a testament to the complex, often contradictory nature of Southern politics, which was a study in paradoxes. Despite his opposition to federal civil rights legislation, for his time, Frank had always displayed a surprising willingness to aid individual Black constituents. Indeed, during Senator Lister Hill's hard-fought re-election campaign, Frank had enough goodwill with the African-American community that he was able to mobilize the Black vote in Hill's favor, leading to a significant turnout that contributed to Hill's narrow 6,000-vote victory.

When he had taken office, the constituency had suffered the quiet desperation of high unemployment and anemic tax revenue. Frank saw it, felt it, and transformed into a relentless advocate for his people's prosperity. He knew jobs were the lifeblood of the region, and he went on a mission to attract industry titans. Vanity Fair Mills and the International Paper Company, once distant names, became anchors in Alabama thanks to Frank's tireless wooing.

With his efforts, the hum of machinery and the steady flow of paychecks replaced the anxious quietude, and Alabama's economic engine roared a little louder. A fixture on powerful committees like Public Buildings and Veterans' Housing, Frank steered federal funds towards public works projects like a legislative sculptor. His clout extended to fisheries and wildlife issues through his perch on Merchant Marines and Fisheries.

But Frank understood infrastructure was the backbone of a thriving economy. He became a tenacious bulldog in the halls of Congress, securing funding for the expansion of the Port of Mobile, planning on making Alabama a vital artery in the global trade network. And then there was the Brookley Air Force Base, the construction pitch of which was spearheaded by Frank to put Mobile on the map. Today, it is known as the Mobile Downtown Airport.

But life still had struggles for the titan to face. The 1962 congressional election saw demographic shifts leading to the loss of his seat to the Republican, Jack Edwards. After this, Frank decided to retreat from the political arena gracefully, retiring to his beloved Mobile. Yet the gauntlet was not yet over; in 1963, Frank Boykin found himself embroiled in a scandal that threatened to topple his illustrious career when baseless accusations of conspiracy and conflict of interest swirled around the Congressman, stemming from a series of land deals in the 1950s. The narrative painted by his detractors depicted a cunning politician leveraging his influence for personal gain.

Several properties Frank had secured in the 50s seemed to be close to earning dividends in 1958, a development firm came knocking, eager to snatch up the Maryland acreage for a staggering $6 million—but the development firm, burdened by unforeseen circumstances, encountered difficulties keeping up with the payment schedule. It was at this juncture that Congressman Thomas Johnson, a supposed ally, intervened. Johnson introduced Boykin to J. Kenneth Edlin, a figure shrouded in controversy within the savings and loan industry. Edlin, sensing an opportunity, proposed a deal that seemed too good to be true—a purchase of the land at an inflated price of $9 million. Ecstatic at the prospect of not only recouping his investment but also turning a significant profit, Frank readily agreed.

The jubilation was short-lived. Edlin, it turned out, was embroiled in his own legal troubles, facing accusations of mail fraud. Boykin, unaware of the depths of Edlin's predicament, attempted to use his political influence to intervene and have the charges dismissed. But Frank's intervention on Edlin's behalf backfired spectacularly. His political enemies, ever vigilant for a chance to exploit any perceived weakness, seized upon this opportunity. Accusations of conspiracy and conflict of interest were hurled at Frank. The narrative they spun was a damning one: a powerful Congressman using his position to influence the legal system for personal gain.

Despite the dubious nature of the allegations, a cloud of suspicion hung heavy over Frank; thus, he was convicted and sentenced to an unfair six-month probation and a fine. It was only in 1965 that a full pardon was bestowed upon Frank by President Lyndon B. Johnson—perhaps in recognition of the man who had performed so great a duty for his country.

Frank Boykin's eccentric, incredible, and unbelievable life came to a close in Washington D.C. on March 12th, 1969, the victim of a failing heart. He was laid to rest in Mobile's Pine Crest Cemetery, though his legacy echoed far beyond. A chorus of structures would rise in his honor over the coming years—the Frank Boykin Towers in Mobile, the Boykin Wildlife Management Area, the Frank William Boykin Highway, and the Frank W. Boykin Elementary School, nurturing young minds in McIntosh. Even academia paid tribute, with Huntingdon College establishing the Frank William Boykin Scholarship, ensuring his name would forever be etched in the halls of learning.

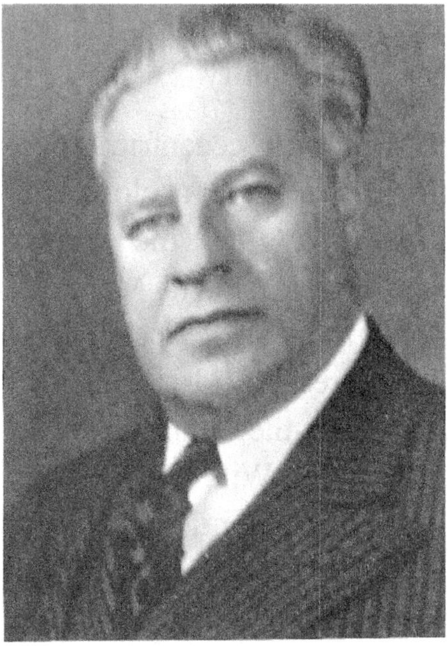

About the Author

Clifford Allen Oxford was born in 1945 in Torrance, California. He served in the U.S. Navy during the Vietnam War era, with assignments on several ships in the Mediterranean and Atlantic. Afterward, Allen pursued a career in real estate, specializing in residential and commercial sales, development, and brokerage in Atlanta, Florida, and Louisiana. He is currently an active commercial real estate broker and licensed insurance agent.

Allen is also involved in marketing CASPR Technology, a pathogen disinfectant that kills viruses and bacteria in the air and on surfaces. He was the first president of the Cottage School in Roswell, Georgia, and has held leadership roles with the Atlanta Jaycees and Rotary Club of Buckhead.

An avid tennis player, Allen resides in Mandeville, Louisiana, and frequently travels with his life companion, Cheryl. He recently completed a book about his great-uncle, Congressman Frank Boykin, and is working on a film adaptation of the story.

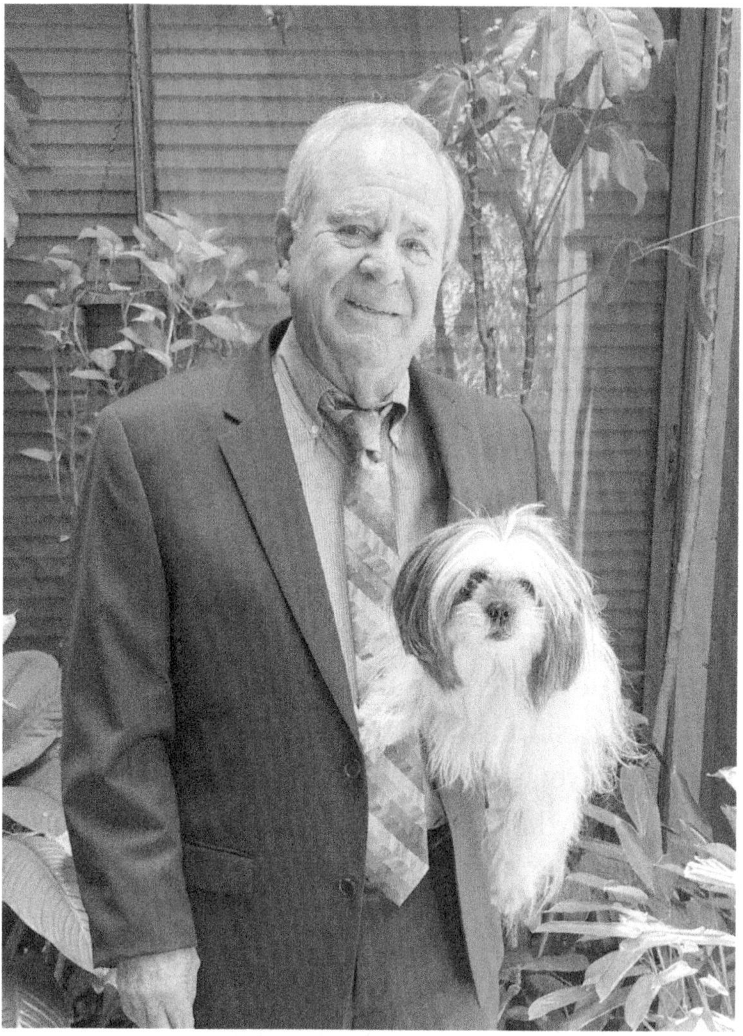

Made in the USA
Middletown, DE
10 January 2025